THE GENERAL

To Ann & Chuck —

Affectionate

greetings

[signature]

Washington, D.C.

May 16th

89

A study of the General in a thoughtful mood taken in Japan,
late 1946.

THE GENERAL
MacArthur and the Man He Called 'Doc'

by

Roger Olaf Egeberg, M.D.

HIPPOCRENE BOOKS
New York, New York

Library of Congress Cataloging in Publication Data
Egeberg, Roger Olaf, 1903-
    The general, MacArthur and the Man He Called 'Doc'.
    Includes index.
    1. MacArthur, Douglas, 1880-1964.   2. World War,
1939-1945—Campaigns—Pacific Ocean.   3. Egeberg,
Roger Olaf, 1903-   .   4. Generals—United States—
Biography.   5. United States.   Army—Biography.
I. Title.
E745.M3E33   1983   940.54'26'0924   83-48634
ISBN 0-88254-854-9

Hippocrene Books, Inc.
171 Madison Avenue
New York, NY 10016

Printed in the United States of America

Contents

Foreword

Nobody has written a book like this about General MacArthur.

That's because nobody could. Nobody else was as close to the General during those tragic and glory years of World War II.

And nobody else is like Roger Egeberg, either. For example, what other Army doctor was seriously threatened with a court-martial for telling off the brass? For example, what other doctor at first refused to be General MacArthur's personal physician? Or his aide-de-camp? Or was made an aide-de-camp to protect him from a WAC Captain too close to a Chief of Staff?

None of these examples, however, paint a full enough portrait of Roger Egeberg. He is tall, red-faced, bald and big-boned. His smile is easy and like sunshine; his anger is not as quick as his smile, and is not at all like sunshine. He is gentle—little children instinctively crawl on his lap. He is rough—the General had a bodyguard with Roger around.

Most of all, Roger Egeberg was and is integrity and character.

I should add he is a damn good doctor, too.

The General must have seen all of this in Roger Egeberg to have taken him so deeply into his own and his family's life.

For years, since the war, many of us who served with the General, have encouraged Roger to write a book about the MacArthur he knew.

Roger said he might someday. We had in mind the personal side of the General. It's a side none of the rest of us knew. And, certainly, none of the authors of the many books about MacArthur knew either.

Yes, there are legions of, perhaps well-meaning military and other folks who talk about "the time Mac and I...." That sort of creative memory surrounds most men of history, just as it fits comfortably into the gossamer tales old soldiers tell about "how I won the war...."

Was General MacArthur really that hard to know?—Not as an officer, not as a commander.... He was what he was, as a soldier—tall, handsome, sure, keen, articulate, with awesome presence.

But there was a difference between MacArthur the commander and MacArthur the man.

As a man, he kept to himself; he was withdrawn somehow, at arms-length, even remote. All of which adds up to being...shy. I hesitate to use the word but that is the way he seemed. Roger, in this book, does use the word, too. However, the General was never "shy" with Roger. Roger was the exception. Roger was almost as close as his family.

In the combat zones, when the General wanted to be alone, he had Roger with him—in a jeep, at a forward position, on deck, at his quarters at any hour. He liked to talk to, or at, or with Roger. Not only as a commander, for he did that, too. But as a man.

MacArthur did that with nobody else.

So Roger Egeberg should write a book—this book.

History needs it; history deserves it. It flows deep in the nature of two men—General of the Army Douglas MacArthur and the man he called "Doc."

ROBERT M. WHITE II
President
MacArthur Memorial Foundation

Norfolk, Va., 1983

Preface

Many writers and speakers have interpreted General MacArthur to us. His thinking, his strategic talents, his personality, the man, have all been laid out and looked at hard. Some have written with scholarly objectivity, others have expressed a degree of unrealistic adulation, and a few would seem to have discovered the man through prejudiced ignorance.

Interpreting someone is pretty much a personal process influenced by one's own individuality and life experience. So in these pages I have left the interpretation of MacArthur to the reader as I describe what I saw, heard, and experienced while with the General for two years, a period during which I became closely associated with him.

The years 1944 and 1945 were important years in the Second World War. Climaxes were reached and the fortunes of war reversed in all theaters of operation. These were the years I served with General MacArthur and became closely associated with him. The Japanese reached the peak of their southern and western advance in the Pacific and were finally turned back at every point. With the exception of a strategically important delay in the Philippine Islands they had swept southward, virtually unopposed, in invasion after invasion, with incessant bombing and rapid advances on land.

Guadalcanal in the Solomon Islands, and Milne Bay and Buna in eastern New Guinea marked the high point of their southward surge in the western Pacific. They were stopped by the American Marines in very heavy fighting on Guadalcanal and by the Australians and Americans in eastern New Guinea. That the Japanese onslaught was stopped some eight hundred miles north of Brisbane was of desperate importance to Australia, where, even after the first American troops had landed, in early 1942, they were still planning to make a stand against the invader along the Brisbane line. On this front they hoped to save the south-east corner of Australia in which seven-eighths of their people lived. This was the situation when General MacArthur was ordered out of the Philippines by President Roosevelt and was made Commander-in-Chief of the newly created Southwest Pacific Area.

At the beginning of the war General MacArthur was in command of our few American troops in the Philippines and of the Philippine Scouts and army. The Japanese had landed in Lingayen Gulf, in the northern part of the most important island, Luzon. With their terrific momentum, high morale, and early advantages they had expected to consolidate their hold quickly on this island and the rest of the Philippines.

These islands were vitally important to the protection of the flank of their proposed life line—the transport of oil, rubber and rice from the southeastern part of Asia which they were then conquering. They had expected to finish their consolidation in a month, before we could recover from the destruction of our Pacific fleet at Pearl Harbor.

Without reinforcements or help of any kind we were eventually defeated on Bataan, to which MacArthur had managed to withdraw most of his Luzon based troops. Corregidor, the island fortress in Manila Bay, was surrendered soon after, but the enemy advance had been held up for three or four important months.

When General MacArthur arrived in Australia, on March 17, 1942, the whole Pacific picture was at its bleakest. The area over which he had just been given command included Australia, the 1500-mile-long island of New Guinea to the north and the Philippines. It also included the Dutch East Indies, Borneo and the Malay Peninsula, 2500 miles from Brisbane. One American division arrived in April, his Fifth Air Force was created in September and the Seventh Fleet became part of his force about that time.

The Japanese advance, though behind schedule, had not

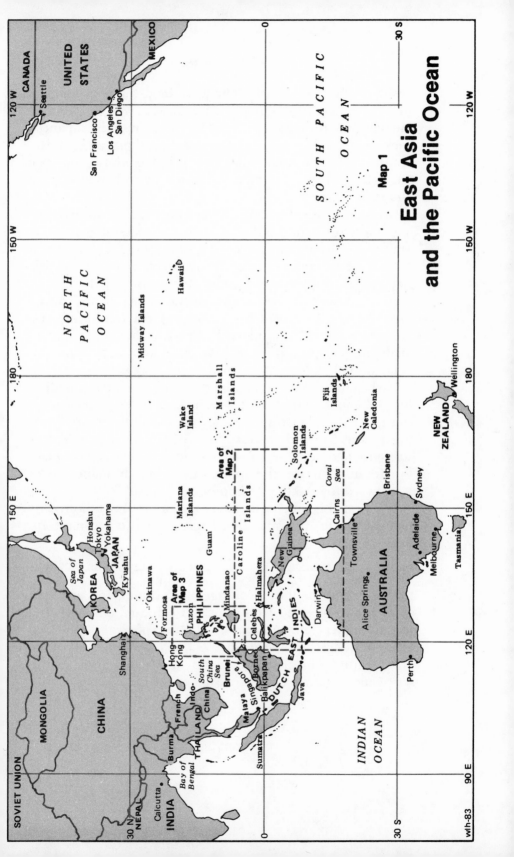

East Asia and the Pacific Ocean

Map 1

been stemmed. He quickly changed the psychology and the strategy to one of defending Australia in New Guinea and the islands to the east, and of beginning to push the Japanese back. He established the General Headquarters of the Southwest Pacific Area (GHQSWPA) in Melbourne on April 18, 1942, and soon afterward moved it up to Brisbane some 700 miles to the north.

During the next 18 months there was a steady strengthening of our resistance to the Japanese, a process in which our Marines on Guadalcanal played a vital part. The Marines, a part of the forces of the previously established South Pacific Area, took a modest air field, Henderson Field, on that island and held that small part of the island against savage Japanese attacks in which the enemy greatly outnumbered our forces on the ground, had control of the air and superiority in local naval units. We had won the battle for Guadalcanal by November 1942.

We began retaking small islands from our enemy, north of the Solomons and started advancing up the New Guinea coast, establishing strong points, building air fields and creating a great forward base at Milne Bay. General MacArthur strengthened our resources, consolidated our gains and laid the foundation for the more rapid and dramatic moves northward toward the Philippines and Japan.

It was at this time, after a year in Milne Bay followed by two months in Australia, that I was invited to become General MacArthur's doctor.

I am grateful for the encouragement, stimulation and criticism I have received from Shirley Cochrane, our once and continuing teacher, and that small group of writers gathered about her. I also appreciate deeply the help of the staff of the MacArthur Memorial Foundation in reviewing the manuscript and in making pictures available to me.

R.O.E.

1

Milne Bay

It was a heavily overcast August day—hot and breathless. The place, Milne Bay, New Guinea; the year, 1943.* A skinny young doctor, informally clad in Army uniform, was driving his jeep on a one-way muddy road above the Gamma Dota dock. One way, *his* way, he assured himself as he saw the six jeeps coming towards him. More of those Sixth Army colonels going the wrong way on their own one-way road. Well, he would show them: just drive into them. He lowered his head but soon thought better of the idea—decided not to hit the front jeep *too* hard, just hard enough to shake up whoever was sitting in it. He looked up to judge the distance and saw on the front jeep a red placard with not one, not two, but *four* stars on it. General MacArthur! He gave his steering wheel a hard turn off the road, jumped out and managed a salute as both he and the jeep slowly sank into the swamp. He watched resentfully as General MacArthur and a large part of the Sixth Army hierarchy, plus some other generals, drove by. Only General MacArthur returned the salute, and the young doctor was certain that he detected a slight smile on his face.

---

*Milne Bay at the eastern tip of New Guinea along with Port Moresby a little farther west, and the hard-fought Solomon Islands 600 miles to the east, were the final reaches of the great Japanese attempt to control the western Pacific. These repulses by the Allies—Australian and American—occurred nine to twelve months after the Japanese attack on Pearl Harbor, Territory of Hawaii, which had brought us into World War II.

I was the young doctor. Even before this incident on the one-way road, I was resentful and exhausted. I'd been going over in my mind bits of the conversations I'd had during the day with the colonels of General Walter Krueger's Sixth Army staff. I had been trying to get a few acres of jungle that lay above the high water mark, on which to base a field hospital. I had found that land, and ten times more, long before the Sixth Army Headquarters had come to Milne Bay.

"Colonel Hagen, I need that land for the 3rd Field Hospital which is arriving the day after tomorrow," I'd said.

"Yes, Roger, you do, and I'm with you, but I'm only the Division Surgeon, so don't put the eefus on me." (I loved the sound of that word *eefus* but never quite found out what it meant.) "Why don't you go around and see G4 (Supply). They handle real estate."

I had gone to see Colonel Adams, G4, and after offering me some land just below high water mark (This difference of a foot or two in elevation made the difference between wading or walking in the hospital tents.), Colonel Adams had finally said, "All right, Major Egeberg, I guess you really need it, but better check with G3" (Plans and Training).

G3 had finally agreed but referred me to G2 (Intelligence) and I had, in turn then, to see G1 (Personnel) and the Chief Engineer. They had all reluctantly concurred, and I was finally on my way back to my own headquarters, beyond Gili Gili wharf, and looking forward to a late supper.

At the time of my encounter with General MacArthur, I had been thinking with resentment of my need to go begging and was in fact talking to myself about the obvious fear these officers of General Krueger's staff had of the old man—the old man sitting in the jeep with General MacArthur.

A half-hour after I steered myself into the swamp to avoid MacArthur, a kind-hearted G.I. with a 6-wheel truck pulled my jeep back onto the road and I continued on toward my own headquarters. My encounter with generals, however, was not over.

I was soon on a road where both jeep and truck could pass and came to a part of it that was continually sinking into the swamp. A truck was at that point backing up to dump some rocks into a low place, so I stopped, but a jeep behind me didn't and swerved around me, blocking the truck and stymying any movement. The driver and his passenger were just opposite me, so I turned and shouted.

"You goddamned, blind sonovabitch, can't you . . ."

At that point my eyes focused on the two stars of a general, who I knew didn't belong to the Sixth Army. I weakly pretended to be cursing my own engine as I backed down the road to a turn. I arrived home too late for anything but bread and marge and went soon to bed still stewing.

I had left the practice of medicine in Cleveland, Ohio, to join the 4th General Hospital, affiliated with the Western Reserve University Medical School, in January, 1942. We had quickly shipped out and landed in Melbourne, near the southern tip of Australia. Since it appeared that we would be stationed there in a beautiful, new hospital for a long time, and the war was being fought several thousand miles away, I managed to get myself assigned to the Office of the Theater Surgeon along with my very good friend, Dave Chambers. We had the opportunity there to evolve the small portable surgical hospitals that could go forward with regiments in country where the wounded could not be brought back very far. After that I managed to get myself assigned to Milne Bay, New Guinea, where I was Surgeon of the Command for our forces of six to eight thousand troops at that time, the Australians having about twenty thousand.

Fall River, as it was euphemistically called in the Army's secret code, consisted of a swampy, hot, wet, steaming bit of jungle with some coconut groves. I had participated in the building up of this base until it became our greatest advance base in the southwest Pacific. I had experienced a modest amount of action and fought malaria and other tropical diseases while being harangued from higher headquarters about venereal disease. After a year's work there, where the temperature and humidity were always above 90, with constant crises at hand, with much fencing to be done with distant headquarters, with a constant shortage of equipment to do the job assigned us, with our Army's poorest rations, with all of this, which we naturally blamed on our Theater Commander, General Douglas MacArthur, I was a bit hard-bitten, very tired, and on the verge of being cynical.

A month or so after this unexpected meeting with MacArthur I was finally relieved as Surgeon of the Command and sent down to Melbourne to be base surgeon there. In Milne Bay I had outlasted four commanding officers and three complete changes in headquarters personnel—and I needed out. After a restful month or so in Melbourne, I was assigned to Brisbane, a rather active base, and it was here that I one day received a call from General George Rice, Chief Surgeon in GHQ, with whom I had worked before in USASOS (United States Army Services of Supply). He asked me if I could drop in on him, which I did, and then he told me that General MacArthur was looking for a doctor for himself and for the officers of GHQ, that he would prefer a non-regular Army physician, a tall man, and a man who had seen some action. If he had added blue eyes and a balding head, I would have been a shoo-in. General Rice said that I was one of three being considered, and that he would like to arrange for me to meet with the General. I said, and with some feeling, "George, I don't want to work for General MacArthur. He's the cause of all my troubles, of all our shortages of equipment and supplies in Milne Bay. I gather he's very aloof, and besides, I've almost enough points to go home."

His answer was pretty clear. "Roger, you're talking awful goddamned big. You go back to your quarters, talk with some of your friends, and come back to see me tomorrow morning."

I did. Of course I returned the next morning, apologizing for my hasty answer of the day before. I told General Rice that I would be honored and happy to serve General MacArthur and would certainly do my best to do a good job, if chosen.

Two days later, I received a call from a Lt. Colonel Allen in GHQ, who said that General MacArthur would like to see me.

"Fine," I replied, "can we set a time for tomorrow?"

"Tomorrow, hell!" Allen said. "He wants to see you today; I suggest you come right over."

Laundry was a problem in Brisbane, a real problem, and I had a shirt from which I'd been unable to completely eradicate some toothpaste, a pair of horrible-looking pants, a disreputable officer's cap, and a belt that, once uncoiled, could have stood up in the corner. I explained my situation to my commanding officer, Colonel William Bleckwin, who lent me his military cap, took off and lent me his own belt, and shoved some shoe polish at me. He then lent me his car and chauffeur and suggested I stop by the quartermaster to try to pick up a pair of pants and a shirt while on my way to GHQ. I did get a pair of pants which I put on in the car en route, but they had no large shirts; so I entered GHQ feeling as though I had been assembled, but not completely.

From Colonel Allen in the Adjutant General's office I was referred upstairs to a kindly looking Colonel Wilson in an anteroom. Colonel Wilson not only looked kindly, he was kind. I had a few minutes with him.

"You're the doctor I heard was coming in for an interview with General MacArthur. You can relax; he'll make you comfortable. Of course, I damn near love him. He reached way down into the bottom of the barrel and brought me out with him from Corregidor. Don't know why—but I didn't ask."

Soon a buzzer buzzed, and, pointing the way to the next room, he said, "You'll now be going in to see the Acting Chief of Staff, General Marshall."

I entered an office where sat a two-star general. I drew myself to attention as my driver had instructed me, and said,

"Lt. Colonel Roger O. Egeberg, 0400-234, reporting for an interview, sir."

I then found myself looking full into the face of the General whom I had called a goddamned sonovabitch in Milne Bay, General Richard Marshall, Deputy Chief of Staff. He didn't smile at all, merely said, "We've met before."

To which I replied, "Yes sir, in Milne Bay, New Guinea."

He looked at me sternly, then said, "I remember. I remember the occasion well." Then after a pause, "Should you come to work here, I trust you will be more temperate in your language."

At that point, he looked over my shoulder, and I was quickly ushered into the General's relatively large office. As I entered, there is no doubt I was a bit unnerved and embarrassed.

The General came toward me in an easy, loose-jointed gait and extended his hand, which I gladly shook. There was a warm smile on his face. The corncob pipe in his left hand gave almost the support of a swagger stick. The informal, open collar, no coat, suited the field of training or of action in Australia and New Guinea. After the greeting, the General suggested we sit down and then asked me to tell him about myself; about a bit of my life, what some of my experiences had been. This was certainly not what I had expected, but I started pouring it out: my birth in Chicago, my education and life in Gary, Indiana, and in Norway; my college, Cornell; a year in India when I was twenty, exploring in the Himalayas; medical school at Northwestern University; teaching; the practice of medicine; and finally, my entrance into the Army through the affiliated unit, the 4th General Hospital from Western Reserve University. He listened, I felt, with interest, asked some questions, and I enlarged on one or two experiences. He suggested we talk more later (which we did), and then told me what he hoped I would do.

"Colonel (I was a Lieutenant Colonel by then), I want you

to be my doctor and if necessary would like to have you take care of my wife, Jean, and our son, Arthur."

I murmured assent, and he continued.

"I also want you to be the doctor for the officers of GHQ." I wondered how many were generals. He continued with feeling, "These officers need a special bit of help. As you know by now, officers in the field, in combat, relieve their emotions, their energy, in action, vent their steam there, through the immediate needs of their comrades and men. In the intermediate headquarters the officers can kick up their heels on Saturday nights and at parties. But the officers of GHQ have neither of these outlets. They are working very hard, long hours with heavy concentration. They get frustrated; they can't show their relaxed side in public. I can see that some are already pretty tense—tired. I am sure some are unhappy. I want you to get to know these officers. Set up a little clinic, or a dispensary, or an office. If they are slow in coming to you—call on them."

Somehow he created the image in my mind that I should walk into a general's office, sit on the edge of his desk and draw him out. I wondered how welcome I would be.

"Get under their skin and find out what they are worrying about. If you think that one of them is near the end of his rope and needs to get away for a week or two, or longer, tell me about it, and I'll do my best to see that it's made possible."

We talked another five minutes or so about the war in general and the work that lay ahead for all of us. Then the interview was over. I left elated. It gradually sank into my head that I had just had a personal conversation—conversation!—with General MacArthur. Definitely a two-way affair. As I left the building I wondered, had I really been offered the job or were there others to be interviewed?

The next day a call from Colonel Allen told me my orders would be cut and I could expect to report for duty in three days. I had been picked.

2
GHQ

February 1944 was a month of building up and planning: the last month before the great-island hopping advance toward Japan. I saw little of General MacArthur. I met him in the corridors occasionally and went in to see him once about a general officer who appeared near the end of his rope from pressures of work. It was a severe and unrelenting stomach-ache that had brought him in to the dispensary.

"Sir, I think General ———— needs very much to go back to the States for two or three weeks." I then gave him a little background.

The General replied, "You know, Colonel, his responsibilities aren't really that great, but he takes them so seriously day and night." After a pause, "If you think he's really played out, tell him to take three weeks. Tell Dick Marshall and he'll tell Fitch." (Colonel Burdette Fitch was Adjutant General.)

As we began to move forward, moving from planning to action or both, the pressures that brought symptoms seemed to lessen, and I had no other patients requiring intercessions.

It was a pleasant month for me, setting up a dispensary, finding a nurse, getting the feel of this general headquarters, and in the evenings gaining personal insights into the power-wielders of the theater with Dave Chambers, Ben Whipple, and their friends.

Dave Chambers, my old friend, and I had shared offices in Cleveland and had come out to Australia with the 4th

General Hospital. We had left the 4th together in Melbourne, and Dave was now the number-one doctor in the intermediate headquarters, named United States Army Forces in the Far East (USAFFE).

Ben Whipple, a young West Point graduate, and a colonel at 28 years, had come out to this theater of war early with a group of technical experts in transportation, construction, lumbering, stevedoring, etc., who had been brought into the Army in view of the undeveloped areas in which we would be fighting. When we met, Ben was responsible for establishing the priorities in all of the intra-theater shipping. We were all three warm, close friends, and were together whenever the opportunity offered.

I was soon given quarters at Lennons, in Brisbane, a hotel used primarily for general officers and colonels of GHQ. Lennons had a prestigious air about it. It was the newest and best hotel in Queensland and the home of all the power and authority of our GHQ. Just to eat a meal there was stimulating to us, wallowing in the brass, as it were. An old courthouse of warm red brick stood across the street and could be seen through the luxurious lavender blossoms of the magnificent jacaranda trees on its front lawn. General and Mrs. MacArthur lived in an adequate but not grand apartment on the top floor of the hotel, where Mrs. MacArthur usually prepared their meals. They never went out socially.

Three or four weeks after joining GHQ, I was invited to a small, rather formal dinner party; formal for me because of the generals who were there, along with an obviously high cut of Brisbane society. One of the officers approached me after dinner and, with an expectant look, asked, "Have you any idea how you got this job, what called you to General MacArthur's attention?" Lowering his voice just a little, "I think he suggested you."

I told him I hadn't the slightest idea; I had thought it was George Rice who had put my name in a pot. He was the officer who had first talked to me about the possibility of my becoming the General's doctor.

"Yes, but MacArthur gave him more than a hint. It was a letter you wrote from Milne Bay, a letter you sent up through channels, on venereal disease. The one Colonel Bland wanted to court-martial you for. Pretty rugged stuff for a major to send to a general, and through channels!" I flushed as I thought of the letter written in a moment of desperation.

"Dick told me someone showed it to the General and it caught his interest. Thought you might want to know—but I wouldn't ask him."

Of course I didn't ask him, but that night I took out the few papers I had kept from the Milne Bay year. It was there, written when I was furious with some unknown stupid character in a higher headquarters. I hardly needed the letter to remind me of the circumstances leading up to it and the sequel.

Malaria was the most serious problem in the command in eastern New Guinea—not just a health problem but a tactical problem, a strategic problem as well because it was overwhelming. The rate was 4,000 per 1,000 per year. That meant everybody was ill with malaria four times a year—some very sick and none were too well between attacks. In six months we had to evacuate a third of our soldiers to Australia. I had tried to get help—work crews—locally, but since every outfit was short-handed, the answer would be, "Look, Doc, I have to unload these ships. I can't spare you any men to dig a ditch." Or, "Sure, Roger, I'd like to help you drain that swamp, but I have to man this ack-ack battery and I'm down to half strength. You were glad to hear our noise last night, I bet."

So with increasing insistence I had pressured the higher headquarters to give me help. Help was simple; oil to cover swamps and pools; more quinine or that new stuff, Atabrine, which was just being talked about; some men for draining; and a little authority. If it were possible we should also move the Papuans of the few neighboring villages farther away. They all had malaria. The answers to all my letters were increasingly threatening messages about venereal disease, with no reference at all to the awesome malaria rate. Our V.D. rate was 8 per 1,000 per year (returned from furlough). This was the lowest ever.

Finally I received a message from USASOS headquarters with that insulting opening statement: "You will reply by endorsement hereon," and which went on to specify, "Do you visit your prophylactic stations late at night?" "Have you obtained cooperation of the civilian authorities so you can apprehend and treat the contacts?" (supposedly prostitutes), and a few more questions equally inappropriate to our jungle setting.

And, what was more, the only females in Milne Bay were among 500 sheep sent up for eating purposes.

That message from headquarters was the final straw. In a fury of exasperation, I fired back a letter faultlessly official in style but in content reducing their inquiries to absurdity. It mentioned the only available female population, which forced the men to choose between "eating the fucking sheep or fucking the bleating sheep," a choice which would work itself out, though somewhat on the order of killing the goose that lays the golden egg. The letter ended with the following words:

The morning drip, the punched-out sore, those swollen, knotty glands have followed up our Army troops to many foreign lands. They come through fun, the Doctors say, supposedly from women. Out Milne way, no amateurs, no whores to take our semen. But forms galore, reports, and charts we have to manufacture so men in higher headquarters can have the facts they're after. If men in higher headquarters could go into the field, we're sure that forms and charts, etc., would be severely 'pealed.

I signed this letter, "Yours hopefully."

A few days after I had sent forward the letter my C.O., Colonel Burns, came running out of his office in the middle of the morning waving a "gram" in his hand. "What have you done now, Roger? What have you done now?" I looked surprised if not innocent, and he read me what he had in his hand. It came from the New Guinea headquarters in Port Moresby and told Colonel Burns to arrest Major Egeberg and to prefer charges against him for the use of obscenity in official communications. When I caught on, I told him of the letter and said I would get the copy and bring it to his office. He harbored similar resentments against USASOS headquarters and seemed to appreciate what I had written, but immediately became serious.

"Who do you know in GHQ?" I told him of Ben Whipple and added Dave Chambers in the USAFFE headquarters. He advised me to send them each a copy, tell them what was happening, and suggest they give it some circulation in their headquarters. I did this and they had shown it, with pertinent background, to several of the high-ranking officers.

Soon Colonel Maurice Pincoffs, our consultant in tropical diseases, arrived in Milne Bay with another medical officer and an epidemiologist. He said the Chief Surgeon thought I had gone off my rocker or was desperate. In two days they heard my story, looked at the statistics and saw in every dipperful of pond or puddle water the countless mosquito larvae wiggling there. They examined the children in one village and found they all had malaria. They went back and reported I had been desperate.

Then three things happened. From GHQ came a directive, a short directive, placing the responsibility for the malaria rate on the commanding officer of each unit. It was just fourteen or fifteen words, but they changed the whole picture. The "eephus" was now on each C.O., the technical advice was in my bailiwick, oil and Atabrine came, and we were allowed to move the inhabitants of three villages.

In the next six to seven months the malaria rate fell from 4,000 per 1,000 per year to 140, and because of the absence of respiratory infections Milne Bay became the healthiest base in the Army.

But back to Brisbane. I had been given space in the Australian Telephone building where the general headquarters was located and went about establishing a dispensary for the officers. GHQ had grown rapidly, and a large share of the increase in personnel had been officers, those needed for planning. General MacArthur's instructions had certainly pointed to the need for a special place to which they could bring their pains, aches, ills and problems.

A dispensary needs a nurse about as much as it needs a doctor. A good nurse can handle so very many of the problems that bring the patients in. She can continue treatment and soon make many of the diagnoses of their more common complaints. But more, and beyond that, in an entirely male headquarters, or virtually so, a warmhearted woman's presence, sympathy, humor and support constitutes a very potent treatment. So I set about finding a proper nurse.

I had a number of suggestions from colonels and general officers who just happened to know some nurses at the nearby General Hospital, and they were good nurses, but I had the appropriate, probably brilliant, and certainly unusual idea of getting a nurse the correct way—through the Chief Theater Nurse.

The Chief Nurse of the American Army—the United States Army in the Southwest Pacific area—was called Ma Clemens. She surely had a first name and she must have had rank, but she was known simply as Ma Clemens. In her late 40's or early 50's, motherly, understanding, able and respected and loved by a tremendous number of people in our theater, she was the kind of woman who nosed around the front in various parts of New Guinea, sizing up situations and getting a real feel for the forward area long before more than a sprinkling of officers from GHQ had gotten up there. I knew Ma Clemens reasonably well, and so I went to her. She was surprised and certainly pleased to be asked to recommend somebody and she promised to have a good and appropriate nurse for our dispensary in a few days.

Two days later she told me of a nurse, a former regular Army nurse, who had married an Englishman in charge of a large lumbering operation in the Philippines, where she was stationed. Their forests and mill were on Mindanao, the large southern island of the Philippines. When the Japanese came, the couple withdrew into the jungle and joined the guerrillas. So they had lived for two years, harassing the Japanese in bloody forays.

The wife had been spirited from the island in a Navy submarine on missions directed by Chick Parsons, a man well known in Manila before the war. The submarine, used for keeping contact with the various guerrilla groups in the Philippines, for bringing them medical and other supplies, and, when indicated, for bringing people away, surfaced one moonless night in a deep bay with a heavily forested shore. It was met by rowboats making the exchange of goods and people; and so Robbie Meers was brought to Australia, possibly against her will, her husband remaining behind to continue harassment and espionage.

When we first met she looked a bit as though she had just been saved from drowning. She was a modest, spunky, happy, hard-working person in her early 30's. I fell in love with her at first sight and so did every officer in GHQ who found his way to our dispensary. She became a virtual drawing card, took care of most of them, and became "Robbie" to GHQ. Many a young officer stubbed his toes trying to get her to go out socially, but much of her heart continued to be in Mindanao with her husband until he was finally brought out to help with our final plans for the invasion of the Philippines.

GHQSWPA (General Headquarters of the Southwest Pacific Area) was a good organization. I sensed relatively little frustration among the younger officers. Their morale, on the whole, was good, though there were disappointments among a few who should have been promoted. Because of the distance of the theater from the Pentagon and the Pentagon's concentration on the European theater they had had to wait months and even a year beyond the normal time when they might have expected a promotion. However, these officers at all levels were busy planning what they knew was going to be an extremely important and long campaign or series of campaigns. They all had much to do and were actively participating in the war, all of which is exhilarating and does raise morale.

I met these officers in the course of their visits to our dispensary or informally of an evening. Since it was not possible to meet Mrs. MacArthur in this way, I was invited up to their apartment to meet her, Arthur and Ah Cheu, the thin, serious prototype of a Chinese amah. I found Mrs. MacArthur to be the delightful, unassuming, and charming woman she was reputed to be. Arthur, six or seven years old, was handsome, bright, nimble, and apparently doing very well with piano lessons. He had few playmates, but he and Neil Watt, the son of the Lennons' manager, were bosom friends. A touch shy, Arthur was definitely likeable.

Left to my own judgment I had decided to remain in Brisbane on Sundays to be available if the General or his family needed me. However, Mrs. MacArthur saw me in the lobby of Lennons one Sunday—alone—and called me up to make sure I wasn't staying in town for their sake. She insisted I not do it, was gracious but firm—and I thanked her.

Two weeks later I was invited to go sailing with Ben Whipple and Dave Chambers. I accepted, had fun in the rigging, got covered with tar and some grease, and came home in the late afternoon to Ben and Dave's billet sun-burned, tired and happy. The phone rang within minutes.

"Mrs. MacArthur would like to speak to you."

"Oh Doc, I'm so glad I caught you. Arthur is sick, has a fever and I wonder if you could suggest what I do?" She thanked me when I said I'd like to come right over. While waiting for a pool car to come get me we surveyed my situation. I started with a shower and then Dave, who was thirty or forty pounds thinner than I, lent me his pants and a shirt. I wasn't sure I could breathe, but I was clean and neat.

Ben unearthed an electric miner's lamp that could be attached to my head, Dave had a thermometer, and I borrowed a kitchen tablespoon.

Thus dressed and armed I arrived at the MacArthur apartment in less than three-quarters of an hour. Arthur looked feverish. Mrs. MacArthur said he had been listless and wanted to lie around all day. I took his pulse, put the thermometer in his mouth and opened up his pajamas to look for spots. None. He had a few swollen glands in his neck, and his temperature was a bit over 103°. His tongue and throat were the next bits of evidence I wanted. His bed was low. Mrs. MacArthur, a little worried, stood on the other side of the bed, Ah Cheu in the doorway. I stooped to have that look and, as I got into the squatting position, Dave's pants gave way with a rending noise, ripping from crotch to the belt in back. Despite this, I had a good look down his mouth. Red throat, no membrane, no Koplick spots, and tonsils not too much inflamed—and then I stood up and backed to the wall.

I had hardly said "Well," when General MacArthur came into the room, almost burst in. I was mentally arranging the things I had more or less ruled out: measles, diphtheria, tonsilitis. It was probably an ordinary sore throat. The General sized things up quickly and advanced on me with an anxious look.

"What's the matter with him, Colonel?"

I could have said FUO (fever of unknown origin), a holding label used in the Army, but I said what I would have said at home: "I don't know." The General's look wasn't comforting, but then he said, "Well, what are you doing for him?"

"Nothing." I was going to add "until tomorrow when I have another look at him," but I just didn't finish. After a few moments during which I was conscious of the draft up my rear and of his piercing look, he suddenly said, "Well, I guess that's right. Thank you."

Of course I did do something. I suggested a salt water

gargle and that he drink much fruit juice. Then I backed out Oriental fashion. The next day his fever was gone and he was fine in a couple of days.

The dispensary was running smoothly with Robbie's great help, and I was beginning to wonder if this were really to be my function, when I got a phone call. It was on the evening of February 23, 1944, and it was from Larry Lehrbas, General MacArthur's aide-de-camp. He asked me to drop over to his room. It was on the other side of the hotel and two floors above mine, but it didn't take me long to get there. Larry was a man of few words and no idle talk, so I thought as I walked over, "Is he sick or is something afoot?"

Larry read a great deal, current literature, a wide range of newspapers, magazines, journals and books, so it wasn't any empty, orderly room that I entered. Aside from Larry, it was indeed full—full of his current reading material and ash trays full of cigarette stubs. I found a chair, moved a newspaper, and as soon as I sat down Larry said, "The General is going on a landing the day after tomorrow and we're going along." Flat out, no drama. A landing! A landing against the Japanese! Landing on a beach! Where would it be? How would we get there, and would we go ashore with the early waves of troops or wait till things had settled down a bit?

First, where would the landing be? Larry professed not to know and said that we would find out in due course. An indication, I thought, that I wasn't quite part of an inner circle yet. Well, what should I take along? The obvious—we would probably be gone four or five days and I was to take the necessary clothes and whatever else I thought I needed.

That was it. I wanted very much to sit around and talk and speculate, to be filled in on the details; but Larry, as was his custom, offered none.

In the past, Larry had managed to be at a number of places in Europe and the Orient when things were happening there. He smelled out revolutions and violent changes of government or invasions and there he would be with an excellent background from his reading, a keen eye, and an ability to get people's opinions and feelings down on paper. Aside from western Europe he knew southeastern Europe, on the edge of and behind the Soviet border. He knew the Middle East and he had lived and worked on a newspaper in Shanghai for many years. With all of this background and experience, and with his conversations with the General he probably had a much better idea than most of us of what our experience was going to be in the next few days, but he wasn't giving out.

I returned to my room elated and excited and finally thought I had better take a walk before trying to go to sleep. This I did, and when I returned I took a look at the clean clothes situation, decided I had better buy another shirt at the PX, a new tube of toothpaste, and if I could get them in my size, several pairs of socks. Then I set about thinking of medical supplies that we would be needing. This was a puzzler, for I was no surgeon, and as I thought of all the surgical possibilities connected with a landing, I felt terribly inadequate.

Then, with these worries and fears running through my mind, it suddenly occurred to me that our transportation would have to be a ship! It would have to have a sick bay and the necessary supplies, equipment, and a surgeon for definitive surgery. That reassured me, and I decided that I would just bring along first-aid equipment and those drugs necessary to take care of the simpler medical needs. So I took to bed, picked up the book for my bedtime reading, an Agatha Christie, and was asleep in three pages.

I saw Ben and Dave the next day, told them I was going to go with the General to visit an installation up north, to inspect something, and would probably be gone for a few days. I later found that Ben, whose operation was in G3 (the Planning Section) was pretty much aware of the landing that we were going to participate in, but he gave me no inkling of it. And Dave, although he wasn't as close to it, had a feeling of what was going to happen. However, they both wished me well, as though I were going to Sydney or Melbourne.

3

Off to the North

February 27th, like most mornings in Brisbane, was clear and beautiful, and the temperature was comfortable—in the 60's. Larry and I met in front of the hotel, awaiting the General, who came down a little before seven. He greeted us with a "Good morning, gentlemen," and we got into the car and headed west, Larry and the General in the back seat, and I sitting up forward with the driver. We arrived at the airstrip, west of Brisbane, on the way to Gatton, in approximately half an hour with no effort at conversation by any of us on the way out. We drove out onto the field and pulled to a stop. There were Hank Godwin, the General's pilot, and his crew lined up looking happy and, I must say, eager. The General's plane, a B-17 which he had called the *Bataan,* had been altered inside but was, nevertheless, a B-17, a good dependable plane, whether for bombing or for passenger use.

Admiral Thomas Kinkaid, the veteran of the Aleutian campaign, exemplifying the image of a fine naval officer, had arrived just before us. After a bit of handshaking we all went aboard. The engines were started, and we were off within a few minutes. (This in itself was exciting to one who had often waited hours for scheduled planes to take off and, on occasion, had to hitch a ride with any plane that had room.)

The inside of the plane, adapted for passenger use, had seats for eight or ten. Twin seats faced one another on the

19

left side of the plane with a few strung out behind and a slightly different arrangement on the right. The General took the front window seat on the left and flew backwards. I had an aisle seat on the same side, but catercorner from the General and facing forward, while Admiral Kinkaid said he had some reading that he had to do and sat across the aisle. Larry, a bit restless, moved about. As we flew north along the coast towards Townsville there was relatively little talk. The land below us was flat, grass and bush, and bright green with myriads of channels and branching streams.

The General seemed to be thinking. I took a book out of my pocket and started to read. My Agatha Christie was in my musette bag, but I hardly thought it appropriate to read a detective story while I was off on a mission with General MacArthur. So the book I pulled out was one I had read several times: Lamb's *Essays of Elia*. I started in on one that I had enjoyed on earlier reading and after a few pages couldn't resist raising my eyes to take a good look at the General. I found him, wrists on thighs, looking at me. I quickly continued reading, and after another page or so looked cautiously up again to find him still looking at me. It was no distant gaze, it was intently trained on me. From then on, the best I could do was to count to about 100 and then turn the page and pretend that I was reading. After what must have been ten minutes and possibly quite a bit longer, he suddenly said, "Doc, what are you reading?" Up until that moment I had been Colonel Egeberg. Something had happened; I had been invited into the informal coterie of a comrade-in-arms. I thought that he must have been studying me and in that quarter hour, perhaps remembering what I had told him about myself at our first interview, had come to feel that he knew me.

I said, "One of Lamb's *Essays of Elia*."

He said, "Oh, which one?"

I told him, "The one about the burnt pig," and he replied that he liked that one, too.

But then he said, "I should think on a trip like this where

you don't know what is ahead of you, that you would be reading a mystery story—an Agatha Christie or something like that." I was still too much awed and surprised to tell him that I had one in my musette bag at my side, and just assured him that I certainly enjoyed such reading, too. After that he looked out the window for a while, slept a bit, and in a few hours we landed in Townsville, 500 or 600 miles north of Brisbane. The General wanted to visit and inspect the large air base supporting our Fifth Air Force.

A forward base had been created here earlier in the war. When, after arriving in Melbourne, General MacArthur had seen the status of our Air Force in Australia, he asked for a fighting, aggressive general to take its command. General George Kenney, able, confident, aggressive, buoyant in temperament, was sent. Whether General MacArthur knew him before or not, he soon approved of him wholeheartedly, for General Kenney acted with swift effectiveness. He found that the overhauling and repair base was in Melbourne, a good 3,000 miles from the fighting in the islands to the north. He sent for Colonel Victor E. Bertrandas, an extremely able organizer, who set up shop in Townsville, on Australia's northeast coast, which was as far north as good supply and communication could reach. Colonel Bertrandas then created this base for the repair and overhauling of all the planes of our Fifth Air Force, and General Kenney was able to get more equipment. Here the unpopular B-25 was adapted for skip-bombing and cannon-caliber firepower, cause enough for the Air Force to be happy with the base.

General MacArthur himself was pleased as we inspected it, large and busy as it was, before lunch. He felt that here was organization. He took to Colonel Bertrandas. He asked many questions which, I gathered from an aside by Colonel Bertrandas, were very pertinent.

After lunch we boarded the *Bataan* again and started off across the Coral Sea. I don't know at just what point I learned that our landing was to be in the Admiralty Islands, about 250 miles off the northeast coast of New Guinea, but I did find out we were flying to Milne Bay, my old home, as it were. There we would get aboard some sort of ship and start north.

Several hours out, the smell of coffee drifted back from our crew's quarters up forward. I knew the General didn't drink coffee, but I asked Admiral Kinkaid if he wouldn't like a cup and, in Navy fashion, he said he certainly would. Larry also wanted one, so I went up forward with our request, and soon afterwards a crew member came back with a small tray with three cups on it. For some reason I jumped up to take them and had just gotten the tray in my hands when we hit a terrific updraft. How many Gs it represented I don't know, but my knees buckled as though they were made of warm wax. The cups went in several directions, one landing on me and another hitting General MacArthur full in the chest. I went down with such force that my rump went through the floorboards with a rending crash that stuck me there in a jagged hole. The admiral and Larry thought it was my bones they had heard break and jumped up to help me. The General, patting his wet shirt, looked at me sympathetically but not anxiously and said, "You're not hurt are you, Doc?" Well, I wasn't hurt, except for bruises, but I was certainly discombobulated for a while. Everybody admitted it had been a whale of an updraft, and Godwin said we had gone up five or six hundred feet in a matter of seconds. I was still feeling waves of embarrassment when we landed in Milne Bay in an hour or so.

Milne Bay—the place I had helped to build up. We were met and driven to the Gili Gili wharf, but it was not the Milne Bay I had left. During the year I had been in Milne Bay, one worked in a thatch-covered hut on stilts, one made one's desk or table out of dunnage one could filch; there were no books, there was no library, certainly no PX, no officers' quarters or non-coms' club, no semblance of a street. Now all of these were here, and I even saw a few people salute. In the five months since I had left, Milne Bay had reached its peak, and that romance associated with modest hardship, continual shortages, frequent obvious crises, the fight with the tenacious jungle, seemed all to be over. The overwhelming malarial infections, the sense of having been forgotten, that feeling of informality and camaraderie under which good work was accomplished—these were obviously gone, and with them the edge went out of my desire to see where I had lived for a year.

Where only jeeps and trucks had been before, we drove down to the Gili Gili dock in a limousine. Admiral Daniel E. Barbey, the commander of the amphibious forces, met us at Gili Gili and we went out to the cruiser *Phoenix* in the admiral's barge, at which time I showed an ignorance of naval etiquette by saying, "After you" to the superior officers. Apparently in getting into a small boat the junior officer goes first and the top-ranking officer last. He in turn gets off first upon arrival at the larger vessel, the idea being that the highest-ranking officer spends the least time in the small boat. In the smooth water the transfer from the barge to the platform at the bottom of the gangplank was easy for all of us. As we were piped aboard, the General and his party were welcomed by Captain A. G. Noble, Commanding Officer of the *Phoenix*. After a few words of greeting, we were shown to our quarters, the General being given the Admiral's cabin, Admiral Kinkaid being given the Captain's cabin, and Larry and I each being given an officer's cabin, mine being that of the ship's surgeon, who said he would sleep in the sick bay. His cabin was down several decks and apparently at the waterline.

Later, as I looked back at this introduction to landings I was surprised that after going through two watertight compartment doors much like tremendous pressure-cooker covers, I had been able to sleep in that cruiser, speeding through enemy waters during a submarine scare.

We hove to in the Finschhaven Roads on the New Guinea coast for the night. After breakfast we went ashore briefly in the Finschhaven area and then crossed the Vitiaz Strait to the Red Beach on Cape Gloucester at the western end of the

island of New Britain, an area very recently taken from the
Japanese by our Marines. The palm trees, the brush, and the
ground looked amazingly bare after a battle and so it continued for a fair distance inland. We walked around and drove
over a few ridges in a jeep, the General visiting rather than
inspecting the area. He could reenact the tactical situation
and did, finally remarking, "They had to fight for this.
They're good fighters and tenacious holders, those Marines."
After a few hours we went back aboard the *Phoenix* and soon
started north.

The General intended this landing as a tactic to save time.
He had been given a large naval commitment from the
Central Pacific Theater for the taking of the Admiralty
Islands, an action planned for two months later. His object
now was to finesse the islands with a very small force and
then to use the massive naval support afterwards for a big
landing on the north coast of New Guinea far beyond the
neighborhood of these islands.* He felt that if he came along
on the landing he could judge for himself, by testing the
enemy now, whether to carry out that idea or to withdraw
and consider this present effort only a reconnaissance-in-
force. He may also have thought that his presence would
boost the morale of the troops, as it apparently did.

Our assault force consisted of the *Phoenix*, three destroyers, and three landing craft infantry (LCI's). Our intelligence had estimated (accurately, it turned out) that there
were well over 4,000 Japanese on the two main islands, Los
Negros and Manus. Our landing force of 500 officers and
men from the First Cavalry Division had already set out for
the islands less than 300 miles away. Since their 10- to 15-
knot craft were slower than ours, we gave them an appropriate lead time.

About nine the General indicated he wanted to turn in, so
Larry and I joined the officers in coffee and small talk for

---

*The plan succeeded. We did save two months in our campaign, and used the
promised large naval fleet to make our landings at Aitape, Hollandia, and Tanahmerah Bay, thus gaining an advance of over 600 miles up the coast of New Guinea.

another hour and then went down to our bunks below, as it were. Even though I had had an interesting and exciting day, even though I had to go through two watertight compartment doors to get to my hot, humid cabin, and even though I would, on the morrow, take part in my first landing, I soon fell asleep.

During the middle of the night, about 1:30, the Marine guard came down to tell me that the General wanted to see me. I dressed—a one-minute job—and went up to his cabin and found him very excited—excited in a peculiar way. Restless, he wanted to move about in his nightshirt, and he recalled, rather emotionally, experiences from his youth, particularly about his years at West Point. He talked of Cadet affairs, about sports which he played, and particularly about baseball. He described one victory that they had, and then he discussed more vividly a defeat, and what to him seemed a moderate disgrace. He talked of these games with emotion, and of his early assignments in the Philippines soon after graduation from West Point; but of wartime dangers, both in the Philippines and with the Rainbow Division in France in World War I, he spoke not at all. I got him to sit down and I took his pulse, which was strong, slow and regular, but he let me go no further with the examination. We sat and talked, and on this occasion he did almost all the talking and I listened for about half an hour while he gradually calmed down, and then rather suddenly said he would like to go back to sleep.

The next morning at a very early breakfast before dawn he was in fine fettle and said in a teasing way, "Doc, you missed that diagnosis last night. I went back to bed after you left and pretty soon I began to feel excited again, so I got up and figured there was something wrong about the bed. Suddenly I realized that at the speed we were going the foot of my bed was several inches higher than the head."

He said, "I just made the bed up the other way, with my head toward the bow, and had a good sleep until I was awakened."

4

Reconnaissance in Force

That morning, the morning of February 29th, could hardly have been said to have dawned. We were up in the pitch dark about 4:30 or 5:00. Out on deck, after our quick breakfast, we gradually noticed a lessening of the intense blackness of night and later a uniform grayness and a drizzle. The cruiser's engines quieted down and we seemed almost to drift slowly in the water parallel to a shore which gradually appeared as the grayness lightened. It was five or six miles off our port side and we could see it better and better. Even the palm trees became visible as the sky lightened into a dismal, heavily overcast morning.

The ship's crew were at battle stations, which seemed to mean they were operating some part of the communications network or manning weapons, from machine guns to 6-inch guns, ready to fire at the enemy, or keeping the whole ship alive and ready. The General was invited to the bridge. He accepted with alacrity, and we went up to join Admiral Kinkaid, Captain Noble and others. In that early twilight I could make out two destroyers and several landing craft infantry crowded with soldiers of the First Cavalry Division ready to go ashore. At that point, I thought they must be wondering pretty keenly about their reception. Cotton was passed around to protect the ears from the noise of the bombardment, which soon started. It was a new and exciting sound for me. No muffled roar, but a seemingly directed explosion—three explosions, then more, some farther away, and then a continuity of them. The cotton did no good. My ears rang in the occasional short intervals between firing, and later, when the shooting was over, hearing was difficult.

The General watched eagerly, intently, as the salvos took off on their six-mile journey from the cruiser's 6-inch guns. As they went shorewards in flights of three, we could see their luminescent rears for an amazingly long time before we finally lost sight of them and then looked for the explosion that would follow on shore. General MacArthur was alternately relaxed and chatting with Admiral Kinkaid or Captain Noble, or watching the bombardment with tenseness and excitement. There was a sudden flurry from the radar room, where the men thought they had "seen" a submarine on the scope. The General thought this interesting but dubious, and it was soon proven to be a very large rock.

We were working our way closer to shore as the hour for the landing was almost on us. There was much talk via phone between the various gun stations and control room. There was an alertness; the ship seemed vibrant. The General was now leaning against the rail searching the shore, looking at the ships of our small convoy, standing on his tiptoes now and then. One caught his feeling of eager interest and anticipation and his strong desire to get in there.

It was now daylight, with a heavy overcast five or six hundred feet above us. Suddenly there was a large splash in the water about two hundred yards towards shore from the ship. I thought at first it was from shorts, almost muzzle bursts. However, twenty or thirty seconds later there was a low rumble overhead and a similar splash occurred the same distance seaward from our ship. We had been bracketed by a shore battery; their next salvo could be expected to land on the deck. There was some scrambling, some crouching, a tenseness in those action stations that I could see, and I was sure this next Japanese salvo would clean those of us on the bridge completely out. A few words passed between the General and Admiral Kinkaid; then the General stood on his tiptoes, grabbed hold of the rail, and took a very hard look at that shore. Just at that point, all of our 6-inch guns, and apparently anything else that might reach that far, let go and continued to send salvo after salvo. Our gunnery officer had spotted the source, figured it out on the grid, and knocked that Japanese battery completely out before they could get their third round off.

We were soon about two miles from shore. One of our scouting planes took off with two bombs fastened under the wings. The pilot, whose job was to observe, look for Japanese positions, and estimate their damage, couldn't resist being more aggressive, so he had wired a hundred-pound bomb on each wing, with an ingenious mechanism for releasing them when he wanted. We watched him go up the coast a half mile or so, turn, and come back, flying low. Suddenly the pilot dived and dropped his two bombs and shortly thereafter returned to the ship. His plane had been hit, but really not damaged. General MacArthur wanted to talk with him, so we left the bridge to do that, moved around a bit, and took a look at the plane.

Back on the bridge, we saw four LCVP's (Landing Craft Vehicle/Personnel), the small landing-craft holding probably 30 or 40 combat-loaded soldiers each, take off from the LCI's and start in to make their landings. This they had to do out of our sight, for they had to go around behind a small arm of the land, which helped make the harbor. They encountered machine-gun fire from the starboard side on the way in, but no frontal opposition as they landed on the beach. They returned and soon a second small wave started in. The coxswain of one of the boats was killed as his boat came into range of that machine gun, and I believe several men were wounded; but they made it to shore. Then, to my surprise, an LCVP came over to pick us up. We were, in effect, the third wave.

The General wore a pair of khaki pants, an open khaki

shirt, and his scrambled-egg cap, so I, thinking I should follow suit, had donned my cap, an ordinary overseas cap. We were told of the machine gun and its location, and the General, as we entered the harbor, could easily have sat down and been well protected by the gunwales of the boat; but he stood up, obviously interested in everything from the handling of the boat to the sweep of the shore. So we all stood. As we passed within a couple of hundred yards of that Japanese machine gun emplacement, I wondered whether, if perhaps I dropped my handkerchief, I might be stooping over to pick it up just at the right time, just as the bullet went overhead; but then, having stooped over, would I have the nerve to straighten up again at any time until the boat reached shore? I doubt those thoughts went through the General's head, for he had turned down a comfortable place to sit as we got aboard, but they did go through his doctor's head. That machine gun didn't fire, our craft hit the beach, the ramp was let down, and we walked ashore . . . just possibly we may have sauntered ashore.

Within twenty or thirty yards of the beach, men were digging foxholes, getting fallen coconut logs into position, setting up machine guns behind them, and, in general, showing a low profile as they approached the Momotu strip, the southeast corner of which was about 100 yards from the shore. General William C. Chase was in charge of this landing force and was already ashore in the first or the second wave. With a couple of officers, he joined us.

With the General leading the way, we stepped over the machine guns, over the logs placed in position in front of them, stepped out in front of all the soldiers who had thus far landed, and started walking up the strip. The General was interested in the condition of the strip, which, as it turned out, had not been severely damaged and could be gotten ready for some use as soon as a few small bulldozers could be brought ashore.

Our intelligence had estimated that there were about 4,000 Japanese on the islands, give or take a thousand or so.

Where were they? The silenced battery, the holes in the fuselage and wings of the scouting plane, the single machine gun at the entrance to the harbor, were all the active evidence that we had had. There were two Japanese just killed, a little beyond the middle of the strip. The General walked over to have a look at them. Although he preferred seeing the enemy dead he had an instinctive respect for fighting soldiers. It wasn't idle curiosity that made him stop. He wanted to see whether they were officers or men, how they were equipped, and if there was evidence of the kind of outfit to which they belonged. However, they were almost naked. At one point we heard the voices of their comrades in the woods just off the strip.

Going up the strip, I had been on the General's left, between him and the far side of the strip. On parade grounds or in cities while walking, the junior man is supposed to be on the left side of his senior. As we turned back I figured maybe I had better stay on that side, the enemy side, and after a minute or so one of the officers remarked rather audibly, "Shouldn't you be on the other side of the General?" The General overheard this and said, "I think I know why Doc is there. This is not a parade ground."

We soon wandered off into the coconut palms in search of shellholes. The General measured them in several places: among the coconuts, in an open area, and on the beach itself. He thought he found the hundred-pound bomb hole and measured it. He later discussed this with General Kenney in connection with prolonged bombardment of the enemy, the plane versus the cruiser's guns.

He then talked with General Chase, about half of whose men were now ashore; they agreed that they should make the perimeter on this side of the strip as tight as possible, for certainly the enemy was already on the other side of the strip and gathering for an assault. The Japanese did indeed make an assault that evening, during which five or six hundred of them were killed on the strip. He told General Chase he would go ahead with the plans to bring up succeeding

Congratulating 2nd Lt. Marvin J. Hinshaw, first man ashore on Momatu Beach, Admiralty Islands, after decorating him with the Distinguished Service Cross. February 29, 1944.

groups of men as fast as the LCI's could shuttle them. He decorated Second Lieutenant Marvin J. Hinshaw, the first man ashore, with the D.S.C. Hinshaw, Jack Sverdrup, "Bing Bang" Bong, our greatest ace, and three enlisted men in the action on Bacolod were the only men that I saw the General personally decorate. He did not like to pin on medals. Perhaps he was aware that decorations miss as many heroes as they find.

We then went back aboard the boat and out to the cruiser to a lunch served on a white tablecloth in the Admiral's cabin, half an hour from that small beachhead getting ready for a bloody attack. At one point during luncheon the General looked at me and said, "Doc, I noticed you were wearing an officer's cap while we were ashore. You probably took a look at me and put it on. Well, I wear this cap with all the braid. I feel in a way that I have to. It's my trademark . . . a trademark that many of our soldiers know by now, so I'll keep on wearing it, but with the risk we take in a landing I would suggest that you wear a helmet from now on."

We stayed in the vicinity for the rest of the afternoon in case there was need for our big guns, then at dusk we turned south to Finschhaven. During the afternoon the General again mentioned the difference in size between shellholes and bomb craters, not denying in the least the need for the shells during the landing, but questioning their ability to further soften a larger area. He was relaxed and happy, sat out on the deck just outside his cabin smoking his corncob pipe off and on. A sailor came up to him and said, "General, sir, would you mind signing my short-snorter?" "Be glad to," said the General, reached out his hand for it and signed it. Short-snorters were legal tender, usually one-pound notes or dollar bills on which soldiers or sailors gathered the signatures of their comrades, their friends, their officers, and when the opportunity presented, some high-ranking officers. Soon two more men came up. "Would the General mind?" He signed and then seemed to enjoy it as the line grew rapidly to twenty, forty, fifty and more. He signed several hundred sitting there in a corner on the deck, and when we finally picked an end point, took forty or fifty additional ones and signed them during the evening.

The General was deeply satisfied with this reconnaissance, his reconnaissance in force, now definitely a landing, and before dinner said to me, "Doc, I am not drinking during the war, but tonight I deserve a little medicine in celebration of this successful reconnaissance in force. Would you prescribe something for me?"

I prescribed some bourbon which was gotten out of the sick bay or out of the bowels of the ship, for liquor is well put away on board a man-of-war, and we each had a drink. It was much more a ceremony than just a drink. As he slowly sipped he talked a bit about the action, then about Jean, his wife. He was also silently thoughtful for a while. This was the only time that I was aware of General MacArthur taking a drink during the war. I knew that he had enjoyed drinking in his earlier days and, I presumed, immediately before the war. He once said that when he was commandant of West Point he had, on occasion, drunk the Assistant Secretary of the Navy under the table, the Assistant Secretary of the Navy being Franklin D. Roosevelt. I asked him about his abstinence and he said, "Doc, I am responsible for all the lives in this theater . . . with others, to be sure, but I am responsible and I think it important that the mothers, or the wives, and the sweethearts of our men, should never get the feeling or have the thought go through their minds that I am the least bit casual about this awesome responsibility. You know I feel it, and I trust they know."

Aboard a cruiser General MacArthur always ate in his cabin, and Larry and I joined him there. If General Kenney was aboard he would join us, and intermittently Admiral Kinkaid might, though he seemed to like to eat in his own cabin or with the ship's captain. On one occasion on our way to make the landing at Brunei Bay, the General suggested that he would like to eat with the officers in their mess. I arranged it. They were delighted, but as the time approached, he quailed, and postponed it to the next day and then the next. He didn't do it. I can only think that he was afraid to eat with them. He was embarrassed and shy. He enjoyed eating with people he knew well, and looked forward to the Generals' mess when he had advanced headquarters in the field, for he knew those officers well; but to sit down with a group of people that he didn't know bothered him very much. He felt responsible for the conversation; he apparently felt conspicuous, and he over-reacted.

We returned to Finschhaven and were met by the *Bataan*. Hank Godwin and the crew flew us across the Owen Stanley mountains to Port Moresby, where we settled into our New Guinea headquarters. These were the offices and houses formerly occupied by the Governor General. General Sutherland was there with a few others of the staff, and they discussed the landing into the night. The discussions were informal, and Larry and I felt free to join in when it seemed appropriate. We talked much of the day before, of its accomplishments, and a bit about Cape Gloucester. We talked about Rabaul, on the northeastern tip of New Britain, and the bastion that it was. The General seemed to feel that with the Admiralties in our hands Rabaul could now be bypassed, to wither, as it were. Both Sutherland and the General felt that they had gained two months in their campaign towards the Philippines and were pleased and satisfied. The talking continued as they discussed points along the north coast of New Guinea: Wewak, Aitape, and Hollandia. Finally, we went to bed.

The next day the General was busy in his office. I visited the local hospital, where the medical staff came mostly from Harvard, and gained some of that reassuring buildup of personal worth that comes with the discussion of problems in which one has a certain degree of expertise.

The following day we returned to Brisbane, stopping for lunch with Colonel Bertrandas at the base in Townsville.

Since the landing I had had twinges of a peculiar sense of guilt associated with our return to lunch aboard the *Phoe-*

nix—white tablecloth and silverware—leaving those five hundred men to face that large impending attack that came during the night.

It bothered me until some time later when I felt very naked on the deck of a cruiser being attacked by kamikaze pilots. On that cruiser, a hole in the ground, even a shallow one, with the enemy coming at me seemed infinitely preferable to that deck.

On the cruiser there was an all-or-none feeling applying to each of the many men working on that deck. We would all have been killed had the plane hit its mark.

5

Between Landings

General MacArthur was elated with his Admiralty Island maneuver. He liked calling it a reconnaissance-in-force, and had explained the significance of this to me again on the way back from Port Moresby. It was its flexibility that intrigued him. There were enough soldiers to make an impact, to draw an enemy response; few enough so they could withdraw if that response was great, but enough to hold until further troops would arrive—if the enemy response should be ineffective. In Port Moresby he had said that this landing, this reconnaissance-in-force, would later be viewed as his brightest maneuver of the war. At that point the second convoy of troops and equipment had already landed, and more were on the way.

During the next three or four weeks I came to see the General in greater depth through others' eyes and experiences.

Normal procedures dictated that all communications with General MacArthur be through General Sutherland. Soon, however, some generals would drop in to the dispensary with pointed hints or explicit messages they wanted me to convey to General MacArthur. Some I did convey, receiving some surprising answers.

Yes, he knew General ——— was a year overdue for a promotion; it did disturb him and he was pushing the Pentagon about it.

Of course he was aware that most of his officers considered
his Adjutant General an arrogant and mean S.O.B. "But he
does his job well; he is a good Adjutant General, and whom
could I take away from any other job that would do as well?
And—you know what I'd get if I asked Washington for a
replacement."

Once, in reply to a suggestion of mine: "You want to
examine me—give me a physical examination? Why?"

"To have a baseline on your physical condition for compar-
ison should you get ill. A normal baseline."

"Ridiculous! My health is fine. I have no symptoms and I
am certainly not going to have any examination!"

A Captain Z came to see me in the dispensary, an Australian woman General Sutherland had brought into our forces
as a WAC captain. He had assigned her the job of reception-
ist in the Telephone Building. This annoyed and disturbed
General MacArthur, who thought more than inappropriate
the presence of an Australian woman, the rank, and the job.
It also nettled him, and he referred to it on several occasions.

Captain Z had been much worried about a symptom to
which she attached undue significance. After carefully ruling
out her fears and reassuring her on several visits, I switched
from reassurance to chiding, which made her huffy.

This useful approach to treatment bounced. Shortly after
the visit General MacArthur called me into his office. Stopping his pacing, he turned towards me and said, "Doc I am
going to make a 'competent' soldier out of you." The word
was *combatant,* but I had thought he had said *competent,* and I
wasn't sure he could do that, so I said, "Competent, yes sir."
Whereupon he said, "I said combatant. I am going to make
you my aide-de-camp," and he pointed his finger at me and
looked serious. I had thought that aides-de-camp were "dog
robbers" who took care of the minor needs or the baser
needs of their general officers. So in a resigned tone of
acceptance I said, "Yes, sir."

The General, annoyed, said, "That's an honor, dammit,"
and clenched his fists for emphasis. After a while and a little

explanation of what aide-de-camp meant with respect to him, he said, "You better go down and tell Dick Marshall right now." I did, and General Marshall seemed surprised, thought awhile, said he would put it into effect right away, and suggested that I had better get some new insignia. I would no longer be in the Medical Corps. The caduceus— the insignia of the Medical Corps, with all its implications— would now be replaced by an aide's insignia, a small red-and-white striped shield with, in this case, four stars across the top. This change of status implied I should carry a pistol when I was with the General in the field and that I should learn to aim and shoot it.

I was intrigued but not quite sure what this change of status meant. Later I learned how it came about. Captain Z had complained to General Sutherland about me; she had been the reason for the transfer of General MacArthur's last doctor; General Sutherland had the power to transfer anybody out of GHQ except General MacArthur's aides-de-camp. The General had got wind of Captain Z's complaint and, having intended to make me an aide-de-camp anyway, had acted immediately to forestall any such removal.

As time went on I came to realize that in making me his aide, General MacArthur had brought me into an inner, inner circle. In this position of broader and deeper trust, I became one with whom he could speak frankly about anything that interested him or that troubled him or made him angry. There were many times when I knew I was a listening presence, but there were also times for conversation or discussion. It became for me a warm association, one in which I learned much in a new relationship.

One day a soft-spoken man called in to see me. "My name is Rhoades; I'm General MacArthur's and General Sutherland's new pilot. I'll be flying the *Bataan*." Major Rhoades, Dusty Rhoades, senior pilot of United Air Lines, had been called to active duty for this assignment. He came into dispensary to see what medicines might be needed in a tropical area under conditions of deprivation.

It gradually dawned on me that he was preparing for a mysterious mission far to the north and west, definitely in Japanese-held territory. I tried to be helpful but felt stymied in thinking of the large potential of tropical diseases. His vagueness in talking about destination and purpose made it reasonably sure he was going to a secret airstrip in the Philippines, one held by guerrillas. This didn't jibe with Chick Parsons' submarine ferrying, from the point of view of capacity or safety.

We met again but I didn't probe. When I didn't see him for a week, I was afraid he was off on a suicidal mission. He then came by again, and I was relieved to find the mission had been cancelled at the last minute.

Though one didn't discuss such affairs, later I learned that the idea of the mission was agreed upon by both General Sutherland and General MacArthur, but the cancellation was by General MacArthur. The purpose, the real values, of such a risk eluded me.

I became increasingly grateful for the cancellation as Dusty and I became warm friends, and later, in the Philippines and in Tokyo, lived together.

General MacArthur trusted Dusty Rhoades. He became part of the family, as it were, and the General always relaxed happily when Dusty was at the controls.

Woody Wilson, the General's military secretary, the man who first welcomed me to GHQ, was going on leave for three weeks, and General MacArthur asked me to take over his desk while he was gone. In this position I had to deal, usually briefly, with all who came to see the General. General Sutherland, when he was at hand, spent a good deal of time with the General talking strategy. General MacArthur felt that Dick Sutherland could bounce a discussion back to him more imaginatively and at the same time with a more solid background than any of the other generals who might have been available. Possibly some of the others were too deferential. He also felt that he had raised General Sutherland in the Army. General Sutherland had entered the Army from Yale

University during World War I. The General had been
associated with him on several occasions and for a relatively
long time in the Philippines. He leaned on him and because
of this did not allow himself enough exposure to the other
generals.

Not many of the general officers of the GHQ came in to
see General MacArthur. They did or had to do their business
with General Sutherland.

There was a modest amount of traffic to General Sutherland's office, and some talks there lasted hours, but apparently he got his work done more in briefings with groups
and certainly on the telephone. General Sutherland was
tough. He was a loner and allowed himself few friends or a
social life. He was considered General MacArthur's hatchet
man, and the question was, did he relish that? I was spared
his hatchet personality, but I didn't think at the time that it
disturbed him to dress a man down or to fire him. He did it
in a flat, on-the-line way—no apologies or explanations, no
softening up, just one or two reasons.

General Charles Willoughby, the head of Intelligence, did
circumvent General Sutherland. He arranged his schedule
to coincide with the General's late hours and liked to stop by
after General Sutherland had left and just before General
MacArthur went home at the end of the four-to-eight afternoon shift. This obvious ploy annoyed the General and he
said on several occasions, "Why don't you explain to Charles
that I understand his maneuver? I know what hours he
keeps, but when I am ready to leave I want to leave." I
explained this to "Sir Charles" two or three times, but he
always said, "I know, Roger, but we exchange a few words
and that is important."

General MacArthur would occasionally ask one of the
general officers, such as Steve Chamberlin, his G3 (Planning), to drop in on him for discussion of a particular issue.
He would receive couriers from the Pentagon, "eyes only"
messages, and orders; he studied his briefings, he read
several newspapers, and he talked. While he was thinking or

talking he often smoked that corncob pipe, but he consistently paced. He had a rather large office in the Telephone Building in Brisbane and could walk 15 or 18 paces along one wall and then collect an additional 10 at right angles to it on the next wall and then retrace. I estimated six or seven miles a day. He would do this with his hands in his hip pockets, or if he held a pipe, with one hand in his hip pocket, the other hand using the pipe for emphasis as he talked.

Aside from the more routine work, General MacArthur received calls from officers newly assigned to our theater in important positions, and not a few civilians came to see him.

Among these callers were Colonel Charles Lindbergh, Bob Hope, a famous churchman, an historian, a well-known sports writer and an occasional fortunate correspondent. The General enjoyed these talks. Sometimes I was present, more often not. He became expansive and he also drew the visitors out. He appreciated their presence and let them know that he was grateful for what they were doing. In the case of Colonel Lindbergh, he listened a great deal. This conversation supported his strategy for going up the New Guinea coast. (I shall mention that later.) But virtually every person, every famous person who came out of his office, men at the top of their fields, whatever they were, would want to sit down in my office. They would always say something along these lines: "My God, he knows as much about my field as I do, or more."

I particularly remember the sports writer saying, "Damn! He knows more baseball and football history than you can find in a book. He knows who won what games twenty years ago. He knows who the champions have been in football and baseball, God knows how far back."

The historian was more reserved, pensive. He just sat and nodded his head after saying, "He was far ahead of me."

Bob Hope was elated and ready to go right up to the front with his entertainment.

Colonel Lindbergh, medium in height, tanned, handsome, looked very much like the Charles Lindbergh who had flown to France alone across the Atlantic some seventeen years before. The General looked forward to their talk. He wanted very much to make one tremendous jump up the north coast of New Guinea to Hollandia in Dutch New Guinea, where there was a large Japanese base. That and adjacent Tanahmerah Bay and Biak Island would be our main objectives in New Guinea before we started island-hopping toward Japan. The Japanese were reported to have several hundred airplanes there, and they obviously had many fair-sized dumps—oil, munitions, food, and so forth. This whole installation needed to be neutralized or destroyed before attempting a landing at that distance. In particular, the Japanese Air Force there had to be destroyed. When the General talked this over with General Kenney on several occasions, General Kenney had said it was impossible to bomb the place because it was out of reach of our fighter planes, needed to support and protect the bombers. Apparently it was 50 to 75 miles beyond their range.

Shortly after the meeting with Lindbergh, the General said, "You know, Colonel Lindbergh thinks he could reach Hollandia in a fighter plane and return. He wants a chance to prove it, and I think he should have it. I'll talk with George Kenney about it." Apparently Lindbergh told the General that if the fighter planes would stay low and go very slowly toward Hollandia they would conserve enough gasoline so they could then assume altitude, perform their mission, and return to our base. The General and General Kenney agreed to let him try it, and Colonel Lindbergh was given a fighter plane, a P-38, and three or four other planes and pilots in addition. They used them on an equivalent run, from Lae, in eastern New Guinea, to Rabaul on New Britain, and when that worked well, our pilots used it on the missions from Nadzab to Hollandia. The General was delighted and most grateful to the Colonel and referred with warm appreciation to the tactic on several occasions.

Between March 28th and 31st, with the fighter cover, using Colonel Lindbergh's technique, we made several heavy bombing attacks on the Hollandia base. The first one caught the enemy so much by surprise that we destroyed the major part of their Air Force on the ground. This turned out to be almost 300 planes. We finished the rest and got several dumps, ammunition, oil, supplies, in the days following.

General MacArthur still had a number of hurdles ahead in selling the long jump to Hollandia to his staff. A minority approved, but the majority were doubtful. He finally decided to override the objectors and to land at Aitape and Hollandia, dropping off the Aitape attack-force as the major convoy passed that point and continued to Hollandia and Tanahmerah Bay. He felt increasingly sure that the Japanese had been drawn well forward and would be expecting our next landing to be at a much shorter distance up the coast from our most forward operation, Saidor. This maneuver, he thought, would shorten our overall time for the campaign by roughly two months, and with the two months he had gained in his Admiralty Islands finesse, he would now be four months ahead of schedule for the assault on the Philippines.

6

Landings: Large, Small, and Great

"Doc, why don't you come along to the briefing tomorrow? You've made a landing, a good one, but you should have a look at what's coming up."

So I joined the General in a briefing about our next advance up the coast of New Guinea. This one was held in a large room in our headquarters in Brisbane—maps on the wall and maps ready to be put on the wall. Twelve or fifteen of his officers were there, primarily from G3. Among three or four rows of chairs, General MacArthur sat in the middle of the front row with General Sutherland on one side of him and General Stephen Chamberlin, his G3, on the other. Younger officers made the presentations of the options; the older ones enlarged on them, asked questions, and joined the more junior officers in attacking or defending the various plans.

Where to land? A two-hundred-mile jump or a five-hundred-mile jump? The Wewak-Hansa Bay area would move us forward approximately two hundred miles, Hollandia in Dutch New Guinea would make a five-hundred-mile advance. After the very successful bombing of the Hollandia air base following Colonel Lindbergh's feasibility demonstration, General MacArthur was in favor of Hollandia, but there was still a majority who felt that it should be Wewak. A

45

little over two hundred miles up the coast from our forward positions, such a jump would be twice as long as any earlier one. Our air reconnaissance didn't show much evidence of Japanese concentration there, and it would be a solid, substantial advance.

The arguments grew stronger. General MacArthur asked a few questions—none that the staff couldn't answer. After three or four hours he said, "Thank you very much, gentlemen," and the briefing was over. There had been several previous briefings, with the issue of *where* always the central focus. We had the promise of a large naval task force for this landing, the one the General had expected to use for the Admiralty landing before deciding to make his reconnaissance-in-force, so the problems of supply and support were not great.

New Guinea is 1,500 miles from tip to tip. The Japanese, as well as we, had to figure out where to put their strength. General MacArthur liked to put himself in the Japanese commander's place. "Now, if I were the Japanese general commanding, what would I expect of us?" He suddenly seemed to ask me this question as we were driving home that same evening. Startled, I didn't have to answer—he did. I was the sounding board. His answer to that question was Wewak, an answer that bolstered his leaning towards our landing in Hollandia. I think he made his decision in the car. He never took a vote on the briefing issues, but asked questions, probed, threw in new possibilities, always ended by thanking the group, and then continued his weighing of possibilities, alone or sometimes with General Sutherland.

On several occasions with me as silent audience he talked in the following vein (I give here only the gist, for I could not remember even on the following day the names of the places and the maneuvers that he discussed): "We can attack at A or we can attack at B. If we do B, which I think we are more likely to carry off, the enemy has at least three alternatives. They can do X, Y, or Z. Now if the enemy does X, we could do A-prime or B-prime. If the enemy does the Y maneuver

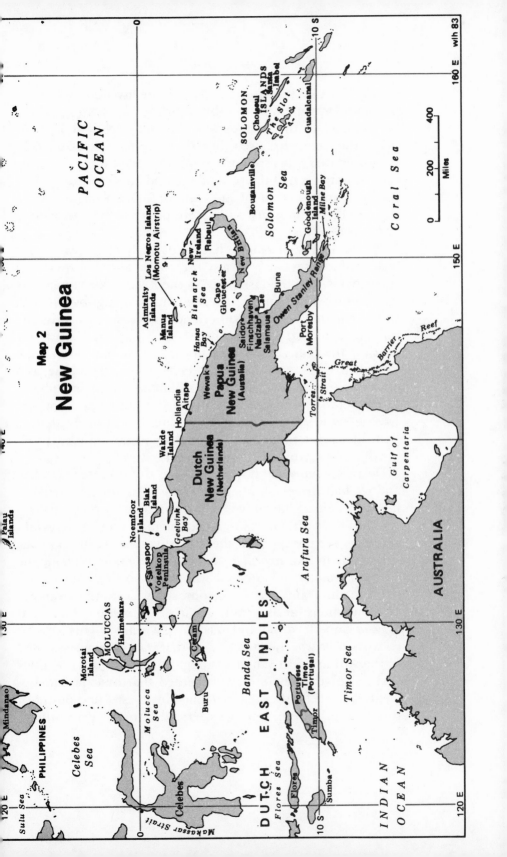

Map 2
New Guinea

we can do C-prime and should the enemy do Z we could perform D-prime and possibly E-prime." As he got excited he changed to the first person pronoun, "Now if I do A-prime the enemy has two things that he can do, X-2 and Y-2." He would carry this scenario of our moves, and the Japanese responses to each of the possibilities and ours in return, all in his head in a period of an hour or more while we were driving, or perhaps just sitting. He pursued the alternatives much as in chess.

It was finally decided that General MacArthur would board the cruiser *Nashville* at Finschhaven and that we would rendezvous with the task force in the Bismarck Sea near the Admiralties. Bent on surprise, General Willoughby, our G2, had persuaded General Sutherland and General MacArthur that we could strengthen the enemy's expectation of our making the short jump by showing great interest in the Wewak area. This we did by P.T. boat probing, bombing, and obvious aerial photography. So, still intent on surprising the Japanese, we would head northwest after joining the convoy. In case we were seen, the enemy would most likely assume that this larger force was heading for Palau, an island well north of New Guinea and a likely target.

Dusty Rhoades had flown the General and his party to Lae and we had driven—over good roads all made by our engineers—to Finschhaven, where we boarded the cruiser *Nashville* and were off. Once we joined the main convoy we would slow down to the speed of the slowest vessel—12 or 15 knots.

For a man like myself who knew little enough about the Army, let alone the Navy, it was awe-inspiring to wake up one morning and see ships, our ships, scattered over the ocean about as far as I could see in any direction. The word *armada* came to mind and was quickly erased. This was the convoy—this was the attack force that was to have been used in the Admiralties. When I thought back to those few ships and those very few men that landed that first day on Los Negros, I was further overwhelmed by the size and power of this group. There were cruisers, destroyers everywhere, landing ships tank (LST), landing craft infantry (LCI), Navy attack transports, APA's, rocket carriers, the aircraft carriers, and some tremendous troop- and heavy-equipment-carrying ships called landing ship dock. Soon the 163rd Regimental Combat Team left the main convoy and headed for Aitape, about 100 miles beyond Wewak, where they made a very successful landing and took the Tadji airstrip the first day.

As we cruised at a 12-15-knot pace toward Hollandia, there was a certain sense of leisure in our small party. General MacArthur enjoyed sitting in a chair in the doorway of his cabin looking out over the ocean and the rest of our convoy. Sometimes he wanted to talk and sometimes he preferred to think. He even nodded, taking short naps. The men with the short-snorters started collecting again, soon forming a long line. The General agreeably signed fifty or seventy-five and then we collected some more for the evening. The short-snorter collectors wanted the General's signature, to be sure, but perhaps more than that, they welcomed this excuse to get close to him and take a real look at him.

When we talked it was never of our forthcoming mission, our landing or our plans. I don't remember discussing the immediate plans on any of our missions. General MacArthur knew that General Krueger and the Sixth Army were out there on those ships. General Eichelberger, with the I Corps ready to land in Tanahmerah Bay, was also there; and the Navy was there in great strength to protect the ships and get them to our objective. But he didn't talk about it. We talked in general terms about people. He once asked me to tell him about the Himalayas near the Tibetan border where I had explored a bit in 1923-24. "What was that country like, Doc?" and "How high did you get?" He asked about the people, where they came from, what they looked like and what the recent history of that area was. Another time he pumped Larry about his experience in Central Europe and anticipating a revolution, on his reason for settling in Shanghai. He might bring up events that had happened long before the war, more of a social than a military nature, and he would often talk about the ship. While he had reservations about the Navy at the top—feeling that Admiral King and Admiral Nimitz were really in strong competition with him, and wondering at times what "bugs" they were putting into the President's ear—he did love the working Navy; he was full of admiration for it. He seemed excited by the cruiser we were on, found it beautiful, graceful, purposeful, and with its guns and its communication center and its disciplined crew he saw it as a very deadly weapon.

We were in communication with our headquarters in Brisbane. The General received a few messages which he read with varied interest and busied himself with replying to some of them. We ate together—he and Larry and I in the admiral's cabin. So went the day at the speed of an LST as we headed towards Palau and then suddenly, with a change of course, towards Hollandia.

At dawn of a day that was to be sunny but hazy, we were in position, strung along the shore much closer than in the Admiralties, probably a distance of two or three miles. Our air support from the light carrier came in and placed a pattern of bombs a little way inland. They made a number of sorties or passes, and then the rocket ships, spaced at short regular intervals, started towards the shore, sending off a continuous stream of rockets. This was the first time that most of us had seen use of the rocket. It was fascinating, and I must say encouraging, to watch. They completely covered the area directly in front of them. The cruisers apparently had targets farther inland and let go with 6- and 5-inch shells.

Finally it was time to land. We all got into the smaller landing craft and soon our men were swarming over the beach and crossing into the jungle. The General landed soon after the first wave. We got fairly close to the shore, were not stopped by sandbars, and didn't have to wade through very deep water. The LST's and other larger boats came in almost at the same time and opened their tremendous mouths,

Signal Corps, U.S. Army

The General sitting outside his cabin aboard ship en route to the Hollandia landing. He enjoyed relaxing in this way, alone or in company. In the foreground: Colonel Larry Lehrbas who was the General's Aide-de-Camp.

Watching the rocket ship's shelling, bombing, and barrage attacks before the landing at Hollandia (Dutch New Guinea) from the cruiser. The author is on the far right in the picture. April 22, 1944.

Signal Corps, U.S. Army

disgorging tanks and bulldozers and half-tracks and other heavy equipment in great volume.

There was little evidence of enemy inland, so the General walked up the beach. Hollandia is within a few degrees of the equator, and even in the early morning it was hot and getting hotter. The sand made heavy going, but the General strode along. At times I thought he was loping—he was hard to keep up with. Of course, anybody who had a camera and caught a glimpse of him joined us. He seemed in better shape than many of the soldiers. He didn't sweat, while they and I were pretty well soaking-wet. At the time I estimated that we had gone a mile or so up the beach, a distance that was beyond our immediate perimeter.

Returning to the vicinity of our own landing craft, we started inland, saw many dumps—dumps of food, oil, equipment, parts for equipment, motors for airplanes, and a very large amount of sake. We visited some of the Japanese quarters—it was rumored that we had captured one Japanese, a general. In the landing we had lost one man, drowned in the swamp as he rushed inland from the sandy shore.

After searching for the effects of our rockets, which, being anti-personnel, had made no holes, but had torn up the vegetation, we watched the unloading of an LST and a huge landing ship dock, then returned to the cruiser and, rounding the Cyclops Peninsula, entered Tanahmerah Bay, about 25 miles to the west. General MacArthur went ashore there to join General Eichelberger and see how his landing in that area was faring. It was going well too, with little or no opposition at that point, and General Eichelberger was happy with the results. He said, with great annoyance, that he felt that General Krueger was breathing down his neck. (And Krueger probably *was* breathing down his neck.)

The day after the landing it was apparent that the initial phase had been eminently successful—we had had virtually no opposition—and were well and strongly situated within rapidly extending perimeters. We therefore returned to

Finschhaven aboard the cruiser and then flew to Port
Moresby, where the General established himself for a short
period in our advance headquarters, before returning to
Brisbane.

There were many other smaller landings along New Guinea's north coast, some difficult, others easy. Taking the island
of Biak at the mouth of Geelvink Bay was the hardest. That
bitterly fought campaign lasted almost two months. Noem-
foor, Wakde Island and afterwards smaller islands up to
Sansapor, the very western tip of New Guinea, were taken.
The Hollandia landing was made on April 22nd and Sansapor was taken on the 30th of July. In three intense months
we had gained control of the entire remaining coast—fifteen
hundred miles of New Guinea shoreline.

On August 11th General MacArthur met with President
Roosevelt, Admiral Nimitz and Admiral Leahy at Pearl Harbor. He wanted finally to persuade the President that the
logical path to Japan was through the Phillipine Islands with
their large land mass and their loyal people, rather than
using the small islands and atolls to the north. He did
persuade President Roosevelt and returned for the final
planning of the Philippine Campaign—or the return to the
Philippine Islands. About the middle of September he did
join the task force that was to take the island of Morotai. The
landing itself wasn't particularly important. He wanted to
get away from the office, where his participation was now
less important, and relax. On his way to a landing the
General was free of his fencing with Washington and the
need to mull over and reevaluate plans and choices for
landings and campaigns. He was, for this short while, out of
contact with the routine matters of his GHQ. He steeped
himself in this freedom and enjoyed it.

Dusty Rhoades flew us to Hollandia, and we drove up the
hill to GHQ offices and quarters on top of a fairly high ridge
overlooking Lake Santani—mountains to the south, ocean to
the north and east, and the lake immediately below. It was a
glorious place. Fishing villages lay here and there along the

The General outside his cabin after the landings at Hollandia and Tanahmerah Bay. April 1944.

At Pearl Harbor with President Roosevelt, Admiral Nimitz, and, back to camera, Admiral Leahy. It was at this meeting that MacArthur persuaded the President to use the Philippines as the stepping-stone toward Japan rather than the small islands to the north. August 11, 1944.

lake shore, many of them completely on stilts over the water. Our headquarters consisted of two pre-fab huts put together in a "T" shape, simply but nicely furnished. The building compared almost favorably with some of the naval head-quarters we had visited. However, General MacArthur was annoyed with General Sutherland for erecting anything but the simplest structure. To top that off, there was Captain Z (General Sutherland's WAC friend) serving lemonade and fruit juices to those coming there on business. It annoyed every officer there to have that particular woman acting as a pseudo-hostess in our forward GHQ. The only woman this far forward, she was not trained for anything of real use to the Army. A nurse or a trained WAC would have been welcome, but even she would have seemed inappropriate at such a time. This was a preposterous irritant, and the General was furious. He asked General Sutherland to have Captain Z sent back to Brisbane.

Morotai, our goal, was a small island off the northeast coast of Halmahera, the large Spice Island of the Moluccas. The landing there was intriguing if not difficult. Its importance to us was that air bases there would protect our flank against attacks from the China Sea when we headed for the Philippines.

The Japanese seemed to expect us in the southern part of Halmahera and they were there in some strength. As we bombarded the coast and spice plantations on the northeast tip before turning back east to Morotai, a great redness appeared in the sky between us and the Japanese position. It was Halmahera's volcano, Gam Konora, in real action. The eruption continued into the day and raised dust clouds high into the sky, later to drift out to sea.

We landed from the *Nashville* on thinly occupied Morotai on September 15th without bombardment. Our landing craft went aground on a sand bar well out and the wading ashore began with water up to our armpits. Admiral Barbey of the amphibian forces was with us and certainly appeared to enjoy *his* landing. During the landing our planes were busy overhead. Small planes, they carried not bombs but a spray. This was probably the first time that the main enemy on an assault landing was insects, insects carrying some disease so far unidentified by us. To me, a physician, this was exciting. I watched those planes sweep up and down in a small formation two or three miles, back and forth. I don't know how often they had to reload, but they kept spraying, ever farther inland until they had covered our expected perimeter of the first two weeks. By then it was hoped that we would have some idea of what we were fighting. I was told later that there wasn't a fly or a bug to be seen for the first two and a half weeks on Morotai. There were some natives on the island farther in, and I learned later that there was a small leper colony there.

A young officer, an observer from the Pentagon, jumped off an LST when its maw opened. With a notebook and pencil in hand, he was ready to take notes on how a well-ordered landing went. Much to his delight, and later I am sure to some in the Pentagon, the first few things to come ashore were brooms and mops, which apparently had been thrown in by some generous, clean-thinking soldier as an afterthought when the LST was being closed up. Obviously, the first things to come off should be instruments of death—guns, and tanks, then bulldozers, then ammunition and oil and so forth, all packed with a view to their successive unloading. These larger instruments did make it to shore right after the brooms and mops.

From the point of view of enemy opposition, the landing was certainly uneventful. We saw no evidence of Japanese or natives, and after walking up the beach and then down the beach for an hour or more, we went back aboard. After we returned to the cruiser, General MacArthur queried me at some length about insect-borne diseases: What might the DDT do? What could such diseases do to people? How quickly would they act? Were they usually fatal or for the most part did they just make people sick? And so forth.

He was intrigued with this relatively deserted island and

very much aware of the importance of an unseen enemy. On the way back he continued relaxed. We returned with one destroyer as escort in less than half the time. The General looked forward to establishing his advanced headquarters in Hollandia.

When we arrived at our headquarters on the hilltop, we were greeted by Captain Z, still serving pineapple and orange juice to the officers. General Sutherland had obviously not followed up on General MacArthur's request that she return to Brisbane. The General became so angry that we flew back to Brisbane as soon as he could get his plane up from Australia, staying only two nights in our new headquarters. We stopped for two days in Moresby, possibly for appearance's sake, for he was not expected back so soon, and then we went on down.

The way was cleared to attack the Philippines. Where? When? My two close friends, Dave Chambers and Ben Whipple, knew, for they were both busy with the planning of the assault. I sometimes spent the night with them at their quarters, but we never spoke about the near and definite future. I had no need to know and I reined in my curiosity, sure that I would learn when the information became pertinent. This disciplined caution, secrecy, applied to other, newer friends from G3 (Planning). We had enjoyable evenings together, but never talked of the impending invasion. This was a way of life, a logical, compartmented work pattern. Then one day General MacArthur suggested I come to another briefing, an overview plus many more detailed operations plans. I then learned when and where. The target would be the island of Leyte—the very heart of the Philippine Island group. He began showing me messages that clarified things further. And I realized I would be there with him when we landed—when he returned.

An air of intense expectation mounted. I was soon aware that we would not return to Brisbane after this. Officers in G3 and G4 were working very late. Some couldn't stay awake; some couldn't sleep. The dispensary became busier with problems of tension. There were a few small parties with an atmosphere of finality about them, though no talk of departure. I was told my footlocker would be picked up by the quartermaster and that I would be taking two B-bags (large duffle bags) with me next time I went off.

Came the morning. It must have been about the 15th or possibly the 16th of October when we boarded the *Bataan* and flew to Moresby and then to Hollandia. After staying overnight there, we boarded the *Nashville*, Captain E. E. Coney commanding, and the next morning found ourselves in the midst of the largest group of ships that my mind could ever dream of. The central Pacific was really putting it on. To the horizon in all directions were ships of all kinds—fighting ships from minesweepers and destroyers to cruisers and even battleships and, of course, transports of every kind. The aircraft carriers were perhaps the most startling because of their unorthodox appearance. I would have guessed that there were at least 500 vessels, but I later learned that there were about 700, so there must have been many beyond the horizon. In addition to generals and admirals, there were several civilians on board one of the cruisers—the President of the Philippines, Sergio Osmeña, and two members of his cabinet. General MacArthur felt their presence in the Philippines on the first day of our landing would signify the return of the Government to the Philippine people.

The two days at sea were much like those on the way to earlier landings. The General was happy, at times very happy. He visited the bridge occasionally, was reasonably busy, usually in the mornings, with the few messages and with their replies, enjoyed his portion of the deck, and worked on two speeches that he was going to give.

He wrote them himself, and the evening before our landing he read to Larry and me what he expected to say to the people of the Philippines and to the world a few hours after we landed. He felt that this was going to be a very important time, a time to rally the Philippine people, to reassure the guerrillas, to warn the Japanese, and to tell the world. There

The bow of an LST, part of a convoy en route to the Philippine
Islands. October 17, 1944.

Map 3

The Philippines

was no doubt that he was going to say, "I have returned."* At
one point, carried away with the rhetoric of an earlier
decade, he had used what to my mind was a terrible cliché.
He wrote, "and the tinkle of the laughter of little children
will again be heard on the streets." I burst out with, "That's a
time-worn sentimental cliché and it stinks." He looked hurt,
defended the wording for a minute, but not very long, then
crossed it out. I certainly didn't use language like that with
the General often, but I wanted to shock him, for this was the
final draft and there wasn't much time. Otherwise the speech
was excellent—appropriate, dignified, and exhortative.

On the morning of the 20th of October any Japanese
stationed on the eastern shore of Leyte below Tacloban who
looked out into the Bay should have been profoundly
shaken. There were most of our 700-ship convoy lined up
along twenty or twenty-five miles of shore. Big guns, smaller
guns, rockets and bombs started pouring in, and there were
at least 60,000 soldiers waiting to come ashore. The knowledge that our underwater demolition experts, those inade-
quately recognized heroes of the war, had been clearing out
the Japanese subsurface defenses for the past several days
was as reassuring as the pounding that the beach was getting.
We were opposite the second landing area from the north.
About five miles south of the Tacloban airstrip, it was an area
which I believe we called Red Beach. We were going in with
the third wave of men, but shortly after the second wave a
rather heavy fog and rain settled in and we waited impa-
tiently for an hour or possibly two before going ashore.

In discussing the talk to the Philippine people the night
before, the General had stressed the importance of President

---

*When General MacArthur was ordered out of the Philippines by President
Roosevelt to take command of the Southwest Pacific forces, he had said to the
Philippine people: "I shall return." Knowledgeable in the customs of the Orient, he
realized that this promise would mean more to them than a statement that the
United States would return, or "Our armies will return." Those in the United States
who disliked the General seized on this statement as being arrogant, and ridiculed
him for it.

Coming ashore on the first day of the landing at Leyte. Left to right: General R. K. Sutherland, Presidente Osmeña, Colonel Lehrbas, General MacArthur, Colonel Egeberg, and General Romulo. October 20, 1944.

Relaxing in a coconut grove with Presidente Osmeña in the Philippines before his famous "I have returned" broadcast to the people of the Philippines and the world.

Osmeña being there and also speaking. He said he wanted me to help "the Presidente," to bring him along with the General. So when we reached the shore, after a fair amount of wading, General MacArthur said, "Mr. Presidente, I would like to have the honor of offering you the help of my personal aide-de-camp while you are ashore here." I then accompanied and led the Presidente to the little clearing where the Signal Corps had set up the microphones. These microphones were to carry the message to a signal ship in the Bay, which would relay it to the rest of the Philippines and to much of the western Pacific world.

In a gentle rain in this small clearing with rifle fire and occasional machine gun fire not too far away, he said, "This is the voice of freedom, General MacArthur speaking. People of the Philippines, I have returned. By the grace of Almighty God our forces stand again on Philippine soil, soil consecrated in the blood of our two peoples. . . . At my side is your President, Sergio Osmeña, worthy successor of that great patriot, Manuel Quezon, with members of his cabinet. The seat of your government is now therefore firmly reestablished on Philippine soil." His speech was short and has been quoted sufficiently so that I need not do so in full.

After he was through, President Osmeña spoke for a few minutes. Then, there being nothing else for the Presidente to do, and certainly no Filipinos around to welcome us, I escorted him back to the landing barge and he returned to his ship. The General, walking briskly down the beach, swung his elbows a bit, and when I rejoined him we went inland, where we soon found some Japanese resistance. After following the perimeter for awhile, encountering rifle fire here and there, the General saw no purpose in our staying longer on this overwhelming invasion and returned to the *Nashville*. He talked little, but the expression in his eyes matched his high color.

The soldiers of the four divisions up and down this coast were working their way inland and meeting a gradually increasing resistance as they crossed the endless rice paddies,

scraggly woods and muddy roads on their way toward the
mountainous backbone of Leyte.

The next morning we went ashore on White Beach, which
was the Tacloban airstrip, a small, pock-marked and poorly
surfaced strip that was to be quite important the day after
the morrow. There were jeeps ashore by then and, with
General Sutherland, we drove all over the strip. General
MacArthur valued the usable remnants of any Japanese
airstrip encompassed within our landings and wanted to see
the strips themselves at close hand as soon as possible. He
wanted to know when this particular strip could be made
ready for our planes. It was in our hands and our perimeter
was well beyond it, but General Sutherland was most unhappy about our spending so much time covering it in a jeep.
He felt, and possibly had good reason to fear, that the
Japanese would have mined the strip. He therefore urged
that we get the hell off it. This possibly reasonable attitude
annoyed the General at the time, though he didn't say so.
However, for the next few days he would worry the idea now
and then, much like a dog worrying a bone. "Why do you
suppose Dick was so concerned about mines?" "Maybe Dick
should have stayed aboard. He's sick." "He should have loved
that feeling of being back on Philippine soil." "What's the
matter with him, Doc?" These statements would come out of
periods of silence during which he was apparently stewing.

On the next two days we landed on the two southern
beaches where the 96th and the 7th divisions had landed,
and we went inland until we reached their perimeters. The
General noted with pleasure the strengthening of the in-
terim shore defenses and the growing amount of equipment
and supplies that were pouring in. He liked having them
come off the ships; it firmed up our initial landing.

On the 23rd, Admiral Kinkaid and General MacArthur
discussed the Japanese fleets, which seemed to be heading
our way from down south near Singapore, from Formosa
and from up near Japan. They could only assume that the
Japanese were heading for the mouth of Leyte Gulf to sink

With General Sutherland in the Leyte Gulf aboard the cruiser
Nashville. Taken before the invasion of Leyte.

our vulnerable troop- and equipment-carriers. We had Admiral Kinkaid's Seventh Fleet and Admiral Halsey's Third Fleet, but Admiral Halsey was under Central Pacific orders and independently had taken his force far north.

On the 25th, Admiral Kinkaid told General MacArthur that there would soon be much naval action at the mouth of the Gulf, that he would have to get down there and that they needed this cruiser, the *Nashville*, in the engagement. General MacArthur said, "Great, when do we start?" He looked almost happy at the prospect, certainly very much intrigued. Admiral Kinkaid's answer was polite but firm. "I am afraid you cannot come along, General. I know you are my boss in the overall campaign, but the Seventh Fleet is my fleet, and this is its flagship. I have to go and I cannot take the risk of your being aboard, so I shall have to ask you to transfer to another vessel if you will, right now." The General looked at him a little while, then with a rueful smile replied, "You're right; we'll get off." And we did, transferring to the *Wasatch*.

That night we could all too vividly see and hear evidence of the Battle of Leyte Gulf. Small flashes, big flashes, lightning-like flashes, the sound of guns, and the explosions of hits, some tremendous explosions, magazines going up. When one thought of the meaning of these sounds, it was horrifying. Information was slow to come to us, and for a time the General was in the dark about the battle's progress. He knew that our whole landing could be virtually destroyed if even one Japanese battleship came up the Gulf. Sitting ducks we were, more than six hundred sitting ducks; our loss of life and ships could be devastating. This could be the end of the Leyte landing—of this assault on the Philippines.

How did the General take this knowledge? Outwardly calm, no damning of circumstances or any person; quiet, yes, but if one knew him one could sense the deep concern he was holding back. There was more and quicker pacing than usual, more frequent pipe-lighting, and a definite withdrawal from us. A few motions of his hands would now and then seem to punctuate a line of thought. He stayed in his cabin much of this time. Finally he learned that the Japanese were using magnesium flares—those very bright and far-reaching lights sent up to come down by parachute. This obviously excited him, and he spoke with intensity: "If they're using flares they can't have radar, and without radar we'll get them in the dark. We'll get them!" He clenched his fist and his face emphasized his words. After that he seemed to relax a bit. This relaxation was a positive indication that he felt the outcome would be favorable, an indication that permeated the cabin with a feeling of relief.

The Battle of Leyte Gulf was an extremely important one for us and for the Navy, and I shall not try to detail what we later heard. That battle, with the glory of the smaller vessels so important to its victory, has been written elsewhere. Suffice it to say that Admiral Halsey, who had pursued a Japanese force—a red herring—far to the north had finally heard Admiral Nimitz's orders and had realized Admiral Kinkaid's plight. He turned south and soon sent planes to the battle, knowing they couldn't return to his carriers. These planes, after their bomb runs, came in to land on the partially repaired Japanese strip at Tacloban and on the Dulag strip twenty miles to the south. The bumpy, shell-torn strips wrecked many of the planes, but they were quickly pushed or pulled off the runway, and more kept coming. Fortunately very few of our aviators were badly hurt by these wild emergency landings. Our cruiser was anchored just off the Tacloban strip, and the General watched at the rail for quite a while as the planes kept coming in. By then he was sure we were winning the battle and tension was gone. I thought there was a look of deep sadness on his face as he watched these brave men, symbols of so many who had saved this day. For my part, I joined several others who wept openly.

7

Leyte: A Milieu for Planning

Leyte went on forever. Heavy fighting, daily bombing, sickness and rain, and death near at hand, week on week of it, mid-October to Christmas and early January.

For us, Leyte was Tacloban and Tacloban was a town of one-story houses in a sea of mud. There was one exception, the large Greek-Revival capitol building for the Province of Leyte near the southern outskirts of town. Tacloban was a place where the sun rarely shone, where the narrow streets and roads were of mud, where the color was gray, where a relatively few good one-story houses in the more central part of town gave way to shacks on three sides and fell down to the docks on the fourth. The people seemed shadows. I saw very few on the streets.

In the middle of the town a large house was found, big enough for General MacArthur's quarters, his office, the generals' mess. It was called the Price House, but Price was gone. A Japanese headquarters had apparently used it before we took over. It was a one-story, nine- or ten-room house, but that one story was on the second-floor level, supported by concrete pillars. Made of brick and mortar, it had a tile roof. Across the street some rubble had been bulldozed away and several Quonset huts were set up for the

75

offices of the advanced echelon of Advance GHQ. Diago-
nally across the street was an open hilly area. Otherwise, we
were surrounded by smaller houses, not unlike the one in
which we lived. The waterfront and the docks were two or
three blocks away. There was a small porch off General
MacArthur's office, fronting on the street and across from
the headquarters. It could hold three or four chairs, but
usually held only two. Behind the porch and back of the
office was General MacArthur's bedroom; behind that, Larry's and mine and other modest rooms serving a few of the
generals of the immediate headquarters, and a very few
visitors. The dining room took up the opposite corner from
General MacArthur's office and was just big enough to hold
a table at which twelve could sit.

We had moved ashore and into the Price House on D-Day
plus six. The headquarters Quonset huts across the street
were just being completed. We explored the General's new
quarters with that eerie feeling that here, just a few days ago,
had been Japanese officers directing the defense (and the
preparation for the defense) of Leyte. Here were their desks
with military papers still in some drawers, their teapots and
their telephones.

In this place and in this environment, General MacArthur
had to plan; had to decide on the next few moves to other
islands. He had to prod and encourage General Krueger
with his Leyte campaign (which included the lightly held
island of Samar across the gulf). He followed avidly the daily
reports from the 6th Army. And he knew the terrain. He
had surveyed and scouted there forty years earlier. While he
rarely discussed tactical details I once heard him say to
General Krueger: "Walter, they should have that hill by now.
Are they getting at the right flank? It has to be weak." From
memory and from maps he knew that hill and the ridges
coming down from it.

He had to further plans for taking the main island, Luzon,
and though he didn't refer to them, he had to start thinking
of the choices beyond Luzon. In addition, he had to defend

The Price House which served as the General's quarters and mess at Tacloban, Leyte.

his plan of campaign from what he considered Pentagon interference. He had to work for the cooperation of the Navy and join with them in planning. Some other commander might have chosen our large advance headquarters in Hollandia, New Guinea, for this work, but now that we were moving in a big way and were in the Philippines, MacArthur couldn't, he really couldn't, go back—and he didn't want to.

So in his office he wrote and read, he received messages and answers. He kept in constant communication with our headquarters in Hollandia and in Brisbane, and certainly with the Pentagon. He would ask officers up from Hollandia for discussion.

The General thought and worried, often alone; but also he discussed with Generals Sutherland or Marshall or Kenney and with Admiral Kinkaid whatever problems were at hand. He might cross the road to the Advanced GHQ echelon to talk with officers who were doing the final planning. But most of his work was in his office. There he would pace, hands in his hip pockets or clasped behind his back, or one hand grasping his long-stemmed corncob pipe. He would pace along one side of the room, then at right angles near the next wall, and back. He particularly liked to pace when he was talking. Not as much space as in Brisbane, and not as many miles, but that exercise was important to his health. He couldn't very well go out to wade in the mud, and he couldn't go out in the country in a jeep. There wasn't much roaming room nor open road for roaming. He would have had to call on a division commander and then go to a part of his "front." It would have taken much time and there were three other divisions fighting their way across Leyte. He couldn't have visited the southern two without spending a night away, and that he couldn't do. So he worked in his office, and he paced.

His concerns were the advancing of our troops, the building of roads, and the repair and construction of airfields. Because of the undeveloped country in which we fought, engineers were probably more important to us than to the

war in Europe—roads and airfields, roads and airfields.
These were both crucial on Leyte, as the airstrips had been in
New Guinea. He was therefore much aware of the problems
and the progress of the engineers' work on Leyte.

Two very valuable generals therefore at these headquarters were Pat Casey, our Chief of Engineers, a West Pointer,
and Jack Sverdrup, his deputy and very close friend. Jack
was an American of Norwegian birth who was surveying
airfields across the Pacific for our government when war was
declared. He joined the Army as a lieutenant colonel and by
the time of the Philippine campaign was a brigadier general.
He had been very active, surveying airstrips during the New
Guinea campaign. He would go behind the enemy lines to
find good strategic sites, or up into the highlands on the
Japanese western flank. He had many of the characteristics
of a Viking—almost light-hearted in the presence of danger.

General Sverdrup ate at the generals' mess, though there
were many occasions when he said he would rather have
gone hungry. But there was one general who was missed
there, and that was General Hugh J. (Pat) Casey, of whom
General MacArthur was genuinely fond. He lived in a house
about a mile from us with a small detachment of engineering
officers and staff who worked with him and with the GHQ
across the street. One may often feel indispensable, one had
heard of people who have been indispensable, but General
Casey was the first person that I heard really labeled indispensable.

The night before our convoy started for the Philippines,
General Casey, in Hollandia, had stepped into a four-foot
hole and badly wrenched his back. He was gotten aboard
ship by his staff and was in severe pain for a large part of the
trip to the Philippines. Soon after the initial landings in
Leyte, Jack Sverdrup had asked me to see Pat Casey, so I
called on him aboard ship and found him indeed in great
pain. The ship's surgeon told me that he had had a setback
with a slipped disc the day before the landing and that he
was immobilized. Though Pat was eager to come ashore, I

wasn't so sure he should; so with his guarded permission I went to talk to the General about it and told him that I didn't think Pat could very well come ashore at the present time. General MacArthur's answer was, "Doc, I don't think I have ever called anyone indispensable before, but at this time Pat Casey is indispensable to me and to this campaign; so you get him ashore and find some way in which he can work." And then to nail it down: "You take care of him so those medicos don't ship him back to Hollandia or Australia."

Those words were good news to Pat, better than any decoration, so we dosed him up with codeine and aspirin and other things that would help his pain, strapped him up, and we strapped him on a stretcher—he was probably the only man who made that landing in Leyte on a stretcher. We put the stretcher on a jeep with the windshield down and in the pouring rain took him over to the house that had been scouted out for him. On his stretcher on the second floor he slept and did his work while Jack Sverdrup covered the island and did his. The only trouble with Pat's place was that during an air raid his staff could seek a lower level, including some slit trenches, while he had to stay there on that second floor and wait to see if one of Bill Marquette's anti-aircraft guns on the airfield across an inlet would follow a Japanese plane to the horizon and pick tiles off his roof, which they did more than once. While I don't believe General MacArthur called on Pat Casey often, he certainly asked how he was getting on every day; and he used him hard, he needed him.

The General was busy in his office with strategy—this campaign and the next—and he talked frequently with General Krueger about progress and hold-ups of this campaign. His main strategic problem, however, was in seeing what he could get out of the Pentagon for the Luzon campaign, and when. During that brief period when he was considered a possible candidate for President and had denied it strongly once, the flow of our supplies and equipment and of new troops had definitely accelerated. The Washington thinking had tended to concentrate overwhelmingly on the European theater. History may give some inkling as to how much of that flow of materiel to us and the acceptance of MacArthur's strategy were helped along by that lurking political possibility. I was not alone, among those who were close to him, in feeling that at that time his greatest goal in life was the winning of this war—the retaking of the Philippines and the conquest of Japan.

Those first five or six weeks or longer, the General rarely left the house. After our early dinners he usually sat on the porch in his rocking chair. He would smoke, but not avidly, and if there was a red alert and he was elsewhere, he would come out to sit there and talk while the officers from GHQ across the street would come out to see whether to duck or not. He liked their habit of first looking to see what might be coming rather than reflexly jumping into a foxhole at the sound of the horn. He might talk of subjects ranging from the Army Medical Corps to our officers in General Headquarters. He liked having me sit out there with him. Sometimes he would just sit in his rocker, rocking gently, and we would have no conversation. Sometimes he would dictate to me something that he was mulling over in his mind, and then ask me to go out and have it typed up so he could see what it looked like. He went to bed early. One night after the General had gone to bed, a Japanese plane flying very low strafed us. The tile on the roof shattered and danced, but two bullets came through a wall and landed in the beam about a foot-and-a-half from the General's head. The next morning he remarked on it—he hadn't gotten up—but suggested we take a look at it and possibly dig one out for him. He thought he might send it to Arthur.

During November the General liked having me move about the country, and I did poke around in my jeep almost every day. I could travel informally pretty much anywhere in the area of the First Cavalry or 24th Infantry Division, the two nearest ones.

"Doc, where did you go today?" or "What did you see in your traveling?" or "What did you hear?"

Such questions usually came when he and I sat on his porch alone after dinner. He listened interestedly, asked questions; or he might change the subject or simply stop me. He often brought up Jean—Jean and Arthur. He felt it was a long time to be away from them at his age. He kept a count of the days since he had left Brisbane.

During a quiet period he would worry and almost wrestle with a new—or an old—problem. The point where the Luzon landings would take place worried him even after the Pentagon had agreed to circumvent the main body of the island and land at Lingayen in the north.

"They want me to go across Samar and ferry across the San Bernardino straits to Legaspi or Tabago! Why, that's where the Japs expect us, and that's where most of them are."

He would sometimes state this as a fact and at other times say it with real emotion. I presumed that in the former instance he thought he had agreement and in the latter he had been challenged. He won the argument—and he was right. After he won the argument, he once came out of a silence—rocking and smoking: "You know, Doc, the way I have to bargain for a few extra days of a carrier's time, you might thing the Navy was almost out of them."

During this period Larry would carefully peruse the newspapers we received and keep the General abreast of world news he thought should interest him. Much of this he did by marking the pertinent articles in blue pencil and then later, when the General had read them, he would discuss them with him. I think the General liked the discussions, but I am not sure he liked having the articles marked.

The enemy bombing that first month was intimate—low level—and the planes strafed us. There was much sickness among both soldiers and Filipinos; tropical disease, polio, hepatitis, leprosy in the streets. And overall there was a sense of urgency. We must build airfields for smaller planes to help the winning of that island, and, hard on these, the larger fields. Those larger fields were needed to support our next big advance, the assault on Luzon, the main Philippine island, with Manila, Bataan, Cavite defended by half a million Japanese soldiers.

On the occasions when he asked General Krueger to come by, they would talk strategy, and often tactics, with respect to the divisions crossing Leyte. Once they visited a Division area in a P.T. boat. Though he knew the very large reasons for it, this slowness of forward progress disturbed the General. The weather here was terrible, but if we could keep close to our schedule on Leyte, we would have good weather for the campaign on Luzon. If a division seemed to be losing momentum he would push General Krueger. With the Japanese coming in from all of southeast Asia in spite of their very heavy losses en route, he finally decided that we needed reinforcements too, and the establishment of a new front. A lateral threat from the southwest coast was made through our landing at Ormoc.

During these weeks, when I would go out in a jeep almost every day, my answers to his evening queries would be varied, and they gave him glimpses—glimpses that he wanted and needed, to sense what was going on about us. I might tell him of a Zero I saw shot down, landing on its nose in a rice paddy, but which was empty when I got there. I might describe a children's ward in the local civilian hospital where there were many emaciated children with large livers and distended bellies who had far advanced schistosomiasis from working and wading in the rice paddies. This was important to us too, because it was in such terrain—rice paddies—that our soldiers were also wading and lying on their bellies.

I remember telling him of two little girls caught in a bombing just a few days earlier, one a six-year-old pointing brightly to the stump of her right leg, and the other, ten or eleven, obviously embarrassed by her own amputation. I described a scene in a small room at our military hospital where a dead-tired corpsman was squeezing a rubber bag twelve or sixteen times a minute, that being the only means of respiration for a young soldier with bulbar polio, whose

The General and General Krueger going by PT boat to visit one of the division headquarters in the Leyte Gulf. December 19, 1944.

anxious look was probably all that could keep the corpsman going.

I told him of a church in a nearby town taken over as a hospital for civilians and military: a large church, three or four hundred cots, the patients a mixture of sick and wounded, many badly so, but with an amazingly good feeling overall of faith that, for the present, within the thick walls of that church, they were safe and that they would all be taken care of soon.

One day I brought back the story of a general hospital from Wisconsin that had gotten news that there would likely be a kamikaze parachute attack in the vicinity of their hospital. Through an enterprising supply man, or one of their officers who believed in being prepared, they had managed to get guns and grenades, and had feverishly dug trenches around their hospital. In the night they had in fact been attacked by parachute troops, and with rifles and hand grenades had repulsed the attack and counted many dead Japanese in the morning. I told him of these things. He might express approval or want elaboration. Sometimes he was silent and at times he would interrupt me and ask a question on some entirely different subject, obviously having had enough.

General MacArthur usually ate breakfast alone. Larry and possibly I and one or two others might join him for lunch. But for dinner he followed a ritual that was accompanied by an enemy ritual. His was to preside at the dinner table with eight or ten generals and Larry and me. These were his intimates. The Japanese ritual was to try to bomb our house at that time.

Almost every evening, and sometimes twice, a Japanese from a southern Luzon airfield would come over in a Zero or slightly larger plane carrying a bomb. He would power-dive us as we ate. These may have been kamikazes, though the pilots did try to get away. The noise of our anti-aircraft firing made talking difficult; the whining, screeching crescendo of the dive-bombing plane hypnotized us. The General might be discussing the war in Europe (never our present problems at dinner), or he might be telling some old Army story on the verge of lore or he might be talking about American politics in a general way. We listened; General Sutherland might respond or question; Jack Sverdrup might have a say, but our thoughts for a few moments were elsewhere. As the firing mounted and the crescendo of the engine began to break through, I would usually light a cigarette to see if I could, and possibly to show that my hand wasn't shaking.

One particular general would freeze, a petrified look on his face. He would stick out his tongue, which was so dry that it carried his upper dental plate out with it, clear out of his mouth. That diverted some of us, and we looked for it as long as he continued to come to dinner. The General might stop talking, waiting for the plane to level off, or for the noise to subside enough for us to hear each other.

There he sat among the men he trusted most. Over half had been in the earlier Philippines campaign with him—the Bataan clan—the others had earned their way into that inner circle. We sat waiting for the leveling-off of the motor's crescendo. It would finally come, the plane a few hundred feet above us, the pilot should have been wounded, but the plane never came apart—and then the wait—one-tenth, two-tenths, maybe seven-tenths of a second—whatever the span, it was a terribly long wait—to see who would receive the bomb, our dinner table, our friends near us, or an empty street. Then the explosion, usually within a hundred yards, sometimes terrifyingly loud, sometimes muffled. And once no explosion. Seconds went by and then minutes. "Well, that one's a dud; but where is it?" We had all heard a bump, but of course each in a different place. The engineers soon found that one—poor engineers!—and disposed of it.

When a bomb exploded I would leave the table to see if I could be of help. I carried a small kit and tourniquet and syrettes of morphine. The tourniquet did save the life of a fellow in that open space across the street—a sergeant who didn't get into a slit trench quite fast enough and had his leg blown off—or I might get a call through an open window, "Roger, Roger, we need some help," and be taken up the street about a block, where there had been a very near miss on a building housing some of our correspondents. Two were dead, and one was badly eviscerated. This man lying there looking at himself turned his gaze to me and said, "Is there anybody here from Texas? I'd like to talk to somebody from Texas." I passed the word to a soldier outside and before we could get the man to a hospital there were twenty or thirty in line to talk with him.

Once our motor pool was the target. A direct hit by an anti-personnel bomb had killed my driver, a fine young Scandinavian with whom I was just getting acquainted.

There were many more: a Filipino rushing out of a house carrying in his arms his obviously dead wife, or a young boy carrying his family out from his house and laying them one by one, all dead, in an orderly fashion on the sidewalk. I could go on and on, for it all seemed to make up that endless time span of the first few months on Leyte. General MacArthur did not want to hear of these happenings. One day, deeply moved, I started to blurt a story out to him. He became distressed and tense: "Doc, don't! They are my men, my people, an innocent people—all my responsibility. Don't tell me these things." He knew and he had seen before, in an earlier war. I daresay that was much in his mind as he constantly tried to figure out how we could do our job with the least loss of life of our soldiers and with consideration for the people in whose country we fought.

8

Leyte II

Among Jack Sverdrup's responsibilities was that of building a larger and more permanent headquarters for us in Leyte. The GHQ echelons were now primarily in Hollandia and Brisbane. A place had been selected near the little village of Tanauan, nine or ten miles down the coast from Tacloban. While our troops were fighting their way into the mountains, making secure the big valley of Leyte and the northeastern tip, and while we were building airfields as fast as the mud would allow, building of the new headquarters had begun—officers' quarters, barracks, and so forth, and a few separate huts or bungalows for general officers.

One day Jack Sverdrup said to me, "By God, what do you think Sutherland has asked me to do?"

From his looks I guessed what, but I replied "What?"

Jack, much exasperated, said, "He wants me to build a cottage for Captain Z down at Tanauan."

I said, "Good God, that's going to make the General look a bit foolish."

Jack agreed vehemently, "I know—he ought to be told."

"Well, why don't you tell him."

"No, I can't tell him, Roger, you know I work under Sutherland. You're the only one who can do it."

I didn't have much question about my responsibility in telling the General about this, since it was such an obvious and visible flouting of his authority, and, beyond that, a demoralizing situation. It was well known that he had told General Sutherland to keep Captain Z down in Brisbane. Larry, who could have broken this news to the General, was visiting aboard ship; so I went in and told him what Jack had said.

He was amazed and exclaimed, "I don't believe it! I can't believe it! I told him not to let her come north of Australia, and he knows that." He became agitated and walked around a bit and then said, "Get me Dick Marshall."

Dick Marshall was more and more taking on the work of Chief of Staff. His office was in the building across the street. So I went out and asked one of the clerks to ask General Marshall to come over. He came in two minutes and went in to talk with the General. When he came out he looked pretty serious. He looked over at me—a touch coldly, I thought— and he didn't speak. In half-an-hour he came back to talk to me.

He said, "I kind of owe you an apology, Roger, for I made a liar out of you. The General told me that you had said General Sutherland was having Jack Sverdrup build a cottage for Z down at Tanauan, and I told him that wasn't true. Now I have just talked with Jack and he says it is true. I didn't know it, but he says he has been ordered to do it. So, what should we do? Shall we go in and tell the General now, or shall we let him think you just passed him a rumor?"

I thought the truth would come out sooner or later, and therefore we didn't need to go in and disturb him with it now; so we let it drop. The General didn't mention the matter again to me; although I had a feeling he gave me an "A" for rumormongering. He continued to want to talk with me in the evenings, and we covered everything else.

The skies became brighter; it seemed to rain a little less; we were getting closer and closer to our final objective of having control of Leyte. There seemed to be less death and destruction and sickness around us. Two general hospitals became established, bringing in much medical and surgical talent and a strong sense of assurance and reassurance for everybody. Nurses came in and a detachment of WACs; Christmas was approaching, and the campaign for Leyte was almost over.

A few days before Christmas, Larry Lehrbas beckoned me into his office. In a shocked conspiratorial voice he said, "Who do you think I was just talking with?" I gave him a chance, and he said, "Captain Z. She's down at Tanauan in that cottage Jack built for her. She just called me on the phone to let me know that she was there, I think."

A bit of conference seemed urgent, so we brought in General Bonner Fellers, the General's military secretary. Larry told him of the conversation and suggested he tell the General.

"Not me, oh, no, no! It couldn't possibly be me. I couldn't do it. I am regular Army. It would ruin my career."

So I turned to Larry and said, "You ought to do it, Larry. You're the more senior."

Larry wriggled a little more calmly, "No, not me. I gave him the last bad news." I don't know what that bad news was, but he and Bonner joined forces, and I was elected.

Reluctant as I was to deliver such a bulletin, I knew it had to be done. I decided to wait until after supper, which was taking place shortly. During a red alert soon after supper, the General, as usual, went out to sit on the porch; I went out and sat there with him. Because it was a red alert, those officers who had been working late, and there were always many, came out into the street. I wondered how I might broach the subject, dreading it, when suddenly I thought of trying mental telepathy. So I asked the General how Jean was, how other things were going, to get his mind off the present scene; we talked about a few other non-war matters and then stopped talking. I sat there and said to myself, "Captain Z, Captain Z, Captain Z," and concentrated on her. I suppose only a minute or two went by before the General said, "Say, Doc, whatever happened to that woman?"

I said, "Woman, what woman, General?"

"Oh, you know, *that woman.*"

"I waited a second or two before I said, "Oh, you mean Captain Z?"

"Yes, Captain Z—where is she now?"

"She's in that cottage I told you about down at Tanauan."

The *WHAT* that came out of the General even startled the officers in the street.

I said, "Yes, Larry spoke to her this afternoon on the telephone."

"Get me Dick!" So I asked one of the clerks in the outer office to get General Sutherland and suggested to the General that I had other things that I should do. He nodded, and I went out as General Sutherland came in.

I went to my room to pick up something and then went down to the street. At the bottom of the steps there was a young guard, rifle slung across his shoulder and fingers in both his ears, for General MacArthur had blown his top, using on General Sutherland a vocabulary that any Missouri mule skinner would have envied. It was a violent, pent-up, end-of-the-rope loss of temper, and it continued for several minutes. The officers in the street below, instead of plugging their ears, were cupping them. The General ended by telling General Sutherland he was to have her out of Leyte in forty-eight hours. There was no doubt that GHQ found that General MacArthur did have a boiling point, and they also found out who their boss really was, for there had been those, though not many, who were wondering whether it was General MacArthur or General Sutherland who was calling the shots.

Two days later Dusty Rhoades took Z and a ton of her personal belongings back to Brisbane.

It would be difficult as well as pointless here to sum up the Leyte operations in any detailed sequence. Four divisions had landed at one time. Each division had its intermediate goals, the attainment of which were all awaited with suspense, and announced by General MacArthur the day they were reached. The fighting became more and more difficult—difficult in the lowlands because of the constant rain, the floods, and the mud. It became very hard to finish the airfields and to get them ready for our planes. In the mountains, where the terrain allowed the Japanese an excellent opportunity to defend themselves, they kept bringing in reinforcements from all the other islands in the Philippines and all the way from Borneo and even from mainland China.

Our planes sank much of their equipment and some of their troop ships, so that they finally had to bring their reinforcements and supplies in by short jumps at night. We also had to bring in reinforcements and had made new landings on the west coast of Leyte, near Ormoc.

Between Leyte and Samar, an adjacent island that the Japanese had not contested, the narrow gulf continued to be full of our ships, which were constantly the targets of Japanese kamikaze planes.

Our campaign dragged on. The Japanese desperately and tenaciously clung to their strong points. We had to use our carrier-based aircraft longer than was anticipated, but finally this amazing, cooperative land, sea, and air assault attained its goal. With our Navy strangling them and with our carrier- and land-based air support giving them no rest as our infantry took the island away from them bit by bit, swamp by swamp, and hill by hill, we finally won control of all of Leyte.

That was the conquest of Leyte, the end of the campaign that General MacArthur had been most eager to announce, to tell our country and the world that we now had much more than a toehold in the Philippines. We had in fact a solid, large base in the center of the islands.

Several days before the campaign could have been considered over, he started writing the announcement, a communiqué to be given to the correspondents. He wrote it himself; he dictated to Larry; he dictated to me. He changed, condensed, polished. He hoped greatly that he could put it out on the day before Christmas Eve, then on Christmas Eve. He didn't want to do it on Christmas; finally on December 26th he issued the communiqué, the essence of which was:

"The Leyte-Samar Campaign can now be regarded as closed except for minor mopping-up. . . . General Yamashita has sustained perhaps the greatest defeat in the military annals of the Japanese Army."

My sympathies went to those who had to do the mopping-up after such announcements, but there was always mopping-up, which took weeks and sometimes months.

Leyte, crucial to the Japanese in their efforts to hold the Philippines, was of course equally important to us in the taking of the islands. But, beyond this, with us in possession of that land mass, the far-reaching Japanese empire could be cut in two, with the oil, the rubber, and the rice in the distal part.

General MacArthur was obviously relieved when this day arrived, when he could say the campaign was closed. It had come ten days or two weeks later than had been anticipated, but it did arrive, and the conquest was accomplished and he became more relaxed, more expansive, and it seemed to me that the sun even began to shine a little more. The kamikaze bombing had virtually stopped a month earlier, and Tacloban was beginning to take on the peaceful, relaxed air of a town in the tropics at the end of the rainy season. He was eager to announce the return of Leyte to civil government and arranged a ceremony with President Osmeña. It was held on the wide steps of the Provincial Capitol on the southern edge of Tacloban at the end of the campaign. A number of our high-ranking officers attended and President Osmeña was accompanied by one of his famous guerilla leaders and a few of his staff.

A few days after his communiqué he told me he wanted to publish an order of the day, which he preferred to talk out to me. I got a pad and pencil, he dictated, and I found out what this order of the day was: namely, an appreciation and thanks to all of those who had participated in the campaign, mentioning some organizations more specifically, and covering others in general. At the end I read it back to him. He thought it was what he had intended to say; so he asked me to take it out, get somebody to type it up, and then bring it back to go over again.

I hadn't gone more than five steps out of his office before I heard him shout, "Doc, Doc, come back here!"

When I came back into the room he said in a somewhat shocked voice, "We forgot God." So I sat down and he included God in his thanks.

That statement may sound strange—on the other hand, it may give some insight into the General's attitude towards religion. Jean MacArthur went to church whenever she could. She knew the hymns and usually enjoyed the service. I attended with her on several occasions. I was not aware of the General attending church during the period that I was with him, yet the General was a religious man. He thought of God as an overwhelming, overriding, unifying force, and felt this force was important to him in his life and to most other people, so he brought Him into many of his talks for the very great mutual good that he felt it accomplished.

The season improved slowly; the mud was not always universal. On Sundays the people of Tacloban and of the countryside about us would put on their clean and best clothes. We would see family groups walking to church. The youngsters even played about a bit. Our headquarters was established down the coast, and headquarters personnel were moved in from Hollandia and from Brisbane. General hospitals were in full operation, welcomed by civilians and troops alike. New airfields were in the last stages of completion or had been completed. With nurses and WACs, there was the beginning of a social life, and our more tender side came out when the WACs gave a large and very successful Christmas party for the children of Tacloban. We could now look forward to Luzon and the next campaign.

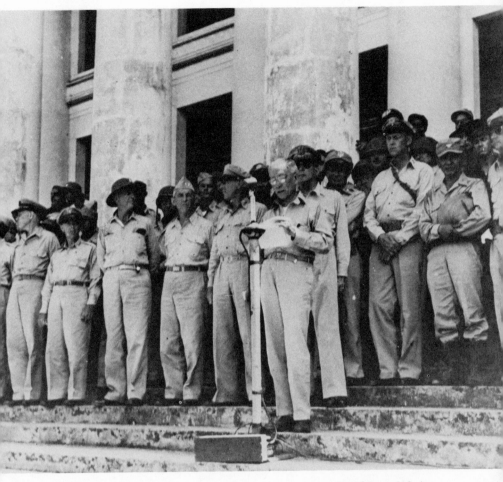

Signal Corps, U.S. Army

At the ceremony announcing the return of civil government to the Philippines from the steps of the provincial capital building at Tacloban, Leyte, late 1944.

9

The Kamikazes

On January 8, 1945, we were aboard the cruiser *Boise* on our way to the exact landing site for which General MacArthur had argued so vehemently. It was twenty miles of beach on the southern shore of Lingayen Gulf in the northern part of Luzon. Our gigantic convoy was coming up the west coast of the island, far out of sight of land, but merely a short hop for land-based Japanese bombers on Clark Field near Manila, 150 miles away. The convoy was being attacked; lead ships were being sunk; and ships' control bridges were being destroyed.

We were under fierce attack by kamikaze planes, each manned by a single pilot whose object was to crash his plane, loaded with explosives, at a target offering the maximum effective destruction. The plane was, in effect, a lethal flying bomb, guided by a man rigorously trained to accept death in this final act. Such a plane had struck Admiral Oldendorf's flagship *California*, killing many on the bridge; six or eight large warships and some smaller ones had been hit, and several sunk.

Kamikaze pilots were expendable, like shells, and were being used in that same deadly way. Was their supply of suicidal men limitless? General MacArthur, as he considered the Japanese targets and thought of the relatively defenseless and vulnerable troop carriers, had said, "Thank God they're after our men-of-war. Most of them can take a number of hits, but if they attack our troop ships so ferociously, I think we would have to turn back."

Earlier on, as we passed the tips of Cebu and Negros, the Philippine islands just west of Leyte, one of our escort destroyers had sunk a small Japanese submarine shortly after the cruiser *Boise,* with quick and expert maneuvering, had evaded two of its torpedoes. As I watched, I couldn't help thinking of my cabin at the waterline with those watertight doors locking me in.

That was an episode. This day was different, with sustained threats, constant watchfulness, hits and sinkings. Antiaircraft bursts far up in the sky showed where attacking planes were. Strings of successive puffs told that they were coming in and hadn't yet been hit. With the naked eye I could see a plane too often; sometimes I could see it blown up in the sky, or with a tremendous eruption when it hit the water.

Far out I saw a puff, the exploding antiaircraft shell that I could never hear. It was high, but I held my breath as other puffs appeared, showing the plane in a steep dive. I thought I could make out its target on the horizon, and a quick look around at that moment showed antiaircraft shells exploding all over the heavens. Dimly, I saw the target, but in seconds there was a tremendous black cloud followed by a second billowing and I knew the kamikaze had made his hit and died with many of our men. My imaging of that moment started to overwhelm me, but new puffs of a much closer plane riveted my attention. The third puff struck it and it plummeted like a hit bird with feathers slowly following. General MacArthur stood up on deck and then sat for a while and watched all of this, avidly interested, twisting his head as the action moved from one part of the sky to another or to the surface of the sea. Each Navy man was intently watching or doing. The General went up on the bridge for a while to hear what they knew. He was told of sinkings beyond our horizons. He paced, he walked about, came back down, stood at the rail outside his cabin and then, later, sat in

The General at sea.

his doorway. He was restless, more restless than I had ever seen him, and he didn't talk. Around him for many miles were 100,000 men trying to accomplish a mission for which he had fought so hard. He had argued first for coming at Japan from the Philippines with their large land mass and friendly, loyal people. Having completed the taking of Leyte in the center of the islands, he had argued hard for this approach to the main island of Luzon. We were going around the island to come in from the north as the Japanese had done three years before. The Pentagon had wanted him to ferry across two small reaches of water to attack Luzon in its southeasterly tip, "and that, of course, is where the Japanese are ready for us."

We now had land mass and we had cut Japan off from its oil, rubber, and food in southeast Asia. We had found a friendly and loyal people—but Luzon would be the climax in the retaking of these islands.

I took a walk along the deck toward the stern, thinking that soft ground with foxholes was much more inviting than a smooth, hard deck during an air attack. I finally chose an anchor chain as the safest place and sat down on it, looking at a ship that had been hit but was not sinking. I was most intent however, on watching the things that were little specks in the sky which quickly and suddenly became large and menacing as they power-dived at us.

Every Navy man aboard that ship had something specific and definite to do, but not I. A few feet away from me, manning a small machine gun, were some men from the mess. Their machine gun range was probably about a fiftieth of the distance from most of the planes, but they pulled their triggers and they coupled that with full and oft-repeated and rounded oaths. Yelling gave them an outlet that I didn't have, and I found myself envying them. I felt alone. Camaraderie was what I longed for.

About then I saw a Japanese plane coming in from the stern at us, at me. It was a couple of miles away, twenty or thirty seconds, but there was no doubt about where it was aiming. Very soon everything on board ship that was intended to fight airplanes turned on it, including my friends. It came on, growing bigger by the fraction of a second, and many pieces of metal flew off its wings and fuselage. The noise of the shooting was terrific, and certainly the excitement was intense. When the pilot was about 400 yards away (2 seconds) he veered, seemed to change his aim to the ship parallel with us and a couple of hundred yards off our starboard beam. More metal came off his wing and fuselage, he veered again, probably not intentionally, maybe even dead by now, and would appear to be coming up between the two ships. As he was almost even with our stern, the tail of his plane came off and it plunged into the water between the two ships. The tremendous column of water and smoke that went up bespoke the large load of explosives that were aboard so the pilot could use his plane as a directed bomb.

This particular event was, so to speak, an intermediate climax. Others occurred, but obviously we were all very much relieved at the outcome of this one, so I went forward to the General's cabin to ask him what he thought of this action. He was lying on his bunk on his back and appeared to be asleep. I couldn't believe it and it worried me, so I stood in the doorway and counted his respirations. They were good—16. Then I went over and took his pulse, a reassuring 68; but my attentions had awakened him.

"What's the matter, Doc?"

I replied, "I just wanted to be sure you were all right and that you really were sleeping. General, how could you sleep with all those guns going off above and around you?" He stretched, rolled over, and said, "Doc, I watched the battle. I watched it for several hours. I got the feeling of it and then decided I had seen enough. There was nothing that I could do that was my business, so I thought I'd catch a little sleep. Why did you say you were taking my pulse?"

That day was a nightmare for many, perhaps for all of our Army and Navy men, roughly 100,000 of them; certainly for the 50,000 or so that passed within range of Clark Field during the day. It finally passed. The night was quiet, and the next morning, January 9th, we woke up in Lingayen Bay. Here was a concentration of ships much like that in Leyte Gulf. We were again landing four divisions abreast, the shore and first few miles inland were being pounded as they had been for at least a day, and we were apparently receiving fire from land-based batteries east of the bay.

On our way toward the broad sandy beach, we looked at palm trees and a few buildings that looked unhurt, no great rubble or destruction. It seemed anticlimatic. We must have seen the worst the day before. There was no enemy, nor did we hear any rifle or machine gun fire. Four divisions, 70,000 men, were landing abreast along these twenty miles of gently sloping shore. What Japanese had been here had pulled back three or more miles from the beaches. Anticlimatic? No. This was what General MacArthur had expected or hoped for, a chance to become well-established, with no threatening opposition. On the way in, he was silent, but before we stepped ashore he said, "We won't be seeing or hearing any Japanese today."

He was right. Our troops came pouring ashore and found only feeble, sporadic resistance after pushing south for four or five miles. With the knowledge that the real action had already taken place, the General soon went back aboard. He suggested I might like to stay ashore for a while. I did; there was much for me to see. With no imminent need for fighting, it was a bit like watching a rehearsal. The men came ashore more like reinforcements. The equipment, supplies, vehicles, and tanks poured out of the maws of the great landing ships.

By luck I met Jack Sverdrup after he had had a little action of his own. He had promised General MacArthur that he would have the Lingayen airstrip ready for our planes seven or eight days after the landing, and since we had taken it early in the day, he wanted to give it a good going-over himself. While he was sizing it up, a small group of our tanks started to cross the strip. Since they could have torn up his field badly and caused him to lose a whole day in repairs, he saw those tanks as a clear and present danger. He pulled out his .45 and waved it and ran toward them shouting and menacing. Finally, somebody stuck his head out of a turret, and Jack was able to get his message across just in time. The importance of having this fragile strip ready by the timetable was obvious. The Naval carriers had to leave on schedule; even one day without air protection could have resulted in vast destruction and jeopardized the entire landing.

General Sutherland had flown up in an amphibious plane and was aboard the *Boise* with the General when I returned. Among other things, I told the General about Jack Sverdrup's actions, to his delight. He was so happy he said, "I'll promote him in the field and I'll give him the Distinguished Service Cross," which he managed to do that day with as much pleasure as Jack Sverdrup must have had in receiving both those recognitions. Needless to say, that was also a guarantee that that airstrip was going to be ready when Jack had promised it, and, with heroic work, it was.

10

The Feel of Luzon

"Doc, don't you like the feel of this open country, the dry weather, and the many people glad to see us back? We're on the main island now, and what we're aiming at is just over a hundred miles from here."

The General was right. This was a very welcome relief after Tacloban. We were sitting on another porch, for the moment just he and I, a screened-in porch of a bungalow belonging to a secondary school in Dagupan, a village a few miles inland in the center of the straight lower end of the Lingayen Gulf. The General, Larry, and I had just finished a quiet, relaxed supper and were enjoying the cool of the early evening in the Advanced General Headquarters which General MacArthur had established in a school in this village.

The school consisted of several buildings, and we lived in a small one, which, judging from the pictures on the walls, must have been the home-economics section. The few offices were in the main building and amply housed our small advance group.

At first the General enjoyed walking about Dagupan. He liked this area; he certainly liked the Filipinos, and he was glad to be here. However, after a few days he found himself leading a parade each time as the Dagupan people, young and old, gathered round and followed him. Some wanted to touch him—or kiss his hand. While he talked with a few, his

107

conversations with Filipinos were usually on his porch, held with people who had been, or claimed to have been, with the guerrillas; or he listened to some of the many who wanted to tell him of those who had been collaborators. There was increasing finger-pointing on that score, and of course the real collaborators were anxious to do their finger-pointing too.

Because he didn't like to lead parades, or was a bit embarrassed after a few, and because he thought it pointless to listen to the accusations of collaboration—which he thought was Philippine business—he curtailed visits unless they were pertinent, and took to his jeep to see the countryside or to visit the areas of Japanese resistance.

One day we had stopped in a small town to the west and he had gotten out to stretch his legs and to look for a landmark of his father's earlier campaign. Soon people came up who excitedly wanted to tell him of the collaboration of a fellow they had dragged along with them. It was obvious that they hoped the General would execute the man on the spot.

We tried to explain that there would be others to take care of such problems and went on our way. After riding a while the General turned and said, "You know, Doc, these people are all worked up and have a right to be when they think of these little collaborators who probably profited or rode roughshod over them when the Japanese were here, but this is and has to be Philippine business." After another ten minutes or so he said as though thinking out loud, "All that I can do is to remove from circulation those who obviously collaborated with the Japanese at the provincial government level or above—and those who did very well financially while the Japanese were here." And that later became his policy.

Our Sixth Army forces were getting established on Luzon. Four divisions had landed simultaneously, the I Corps with the 43rd and 6th Divisions on the east and the XIV Corps with the 40th and 37th Divisions on the west. The resistance on the beach had been nonexistent, but it was firming up as we pressed south, and particularly so to the east and north-

MacArthur Memorial Foundation

General MacArthur's quarters at Dagupan, Northern Luzon.

Stretching his legs in Dagupan, Luzon—the General leads
the "parade."

MacArthur Memorial Foundation

east of us where the roads into the mountains were being strongly held.

The broad plain of the central valley stretched southward to Manila, a hundred and ten or twenty miles away. The country was flat farmland with rice fields all about us and large shallow ponds for the cultivation of fish.

The engineers were working feverishly to get the local airfield repaired and enlarged and ready for our fighter planes by six to eight days after the landing, for that was when the Navy was scheduled to withdraw its carrier support. This was the airfield the General needed badly on a specific day. It was the field Jack Sverdrup had saved from our tanks on the day of landing, as I have already explained. The General had called Jack in to that other porch on Leyte weeks before we had started for our Luzon landing. Jack had studied our reconnaissance pictures, knew what the convoy would bring in, knew the fighter planes that would have to take off and land there, and had a rough idea of when the second field might be ready. I happened to be on the porch at the time. In the course of the short conversation we moved in to the General's office, for he wanted to pace. He said, "Jack, I can't talk the Navy or the Pentagon out of another day's carrier support beyond D plus seven. I think they believe the Japanese would organize, bring in some bombers to Clark Field or the Cagayan Valley and attack them. Can you get that small field the Japanese are using at Lingayan ready for George's [General George Kenney] fighters by D plus seven?"

General MacArthur looked stern as he asked the question; a very important question for the security of our landing. Jack waited two or three seconds (he had his sense of drama too); then, using his forefinger for emphasis and exuding confidence, he took a step forward and said, "You'll have it, sir." The General stopped pacing—they looked at each other. Finally he said, "Great! Great!" looked relieved, and began to relax. He knew that, given a successful landing, he would indeed have that strip when Jack promised.

The feeling pervading our small headquarters was far from tense. The responsibility at this stage, barring catastrophe, was certainly General Krueger's and his corps commanders'.

Dagupan's unpaved streets were wide, open, and lined with flowering shrubs and bushes, and there were palm trees about. The modest houses had large screened-in porches, the small ones none. The season, now dry and without mud, contributed to our sense that we had a clean, fresh slate. We held the central Philippines, the Japanese could not bring in further reinforcements, and they did not bomb us. For all of these reasons we were happier, and Dagupan was infinitely different from Tacloban.

The General avidly read the reports that came up through corps and Army about the fighting on Luzon and, of course, was in constant touch with the rest of the general headquarters which he was anxious to consolidate. He wanted to know where the enemy was strongest and where they seemed more willing to give way. The resistance was strong to the east and north, the Japanese appearing particularly stubborn about Damortis, ten or twelve miles northeast of Dagupan. The Japanese obviously did not want to give up the routes into and through the mountains to the Cagayan Valley northeast of us.

As the fighting became rugged around Damortis, the General decided to visit the area. General Hanford McNider was pushing along Route 11 towards Rosario and Baguio with the 158th Regimental Combat Team. We started off in the jeep, the General in the right front seat holding on to the windshield post to brace himself, I alone in the back. We drove along through open country and rather loose woods, certainly not jungle, and saw no Filipinos on the road.

Soon there were occasional shells exploding in our general vicinity, sporadic, either side of the road, and now and then on the road, perhaps a half mile ahead of us. As we came closer to the area they were peppering, the tempo of the firing increased, and just at that point the General called,

"Stop!" in a loud and certainly authoritative voice. I knew from earlier experience it wasn't the shell-bursts that had brought this on, and I soon found out what.

"Drive over there," said the General, and we crossed the road to where there was a cannon stuck mouth-down into a large block of concrete. The General turned around and touched my chest with his finger.

"On that spot, Doc, about forty-five years ago, my father's aide-de-camp was killed standing at his side." He poked my chest a few more times and then seemed lost in thought. Since he liked the idea of historic repetition, I wondered whether he thought that I might at least get wounded at his side? It was finally I who said to the driver, "Let's get the hell out of here." So we continued along the road going north-ward. The shelling became sporadic again, and we were soon beyond it.

The road was fairly well paved, a good road, often tree-lined, occasionally in full view of the gulf, and then inland a little way, but staying on the coastal plain. Here and there was something of ours; a small oil dump or a pile of boxes or crates, a tent, some guarded, some not; and suddenly in a small wood, as we rounded a turn, there lay eight black thick discs across the road. These were land mines, and this was the end of our road. Guards, appearing on either side, told us that General McNider's headquarters were back down the road just a little way. We turned back and passed a small outfit with several tents—a portable surgical hospital, one of those very small units capable of giving definitive surgery right there, wonderful for the morale of a regiment or a division in action. A doctor I knew well, Bill Garlic, was running this one, which had been shelled during the night with some ripping of tents and a few casualties.

We finally found General McNider, who had just discov-ered why his troops had not been moving inland faster. As he often did, he had gone forward to see "why the hell" they weren't. The Japanese had answered the question with heavy machine-gun fire and had almost gotten him. General

MacArthur and he talked for an hour or so standing by the jeep or moving around. Later we walked up to the roadblock; General MacArthur took a look at General McNider's map to see what was just beyond this little wood, looked longingly into it, finally said goodbye, and came back and got into his jeep. We returned the way we had come. The trip home was more quiet, and we scooted past the cannon, muzzle-down in the block of cement.

The next morning General Sutherland came by in his jeep. The General came out to talk with him. In a minute or so General Sutherland said he had a bad toothache and was flying back to one of the general hospitals on Leyte to see if they could take care of it. General MacArthur sounded concerned and sympathetic; then just as his jeep started, Sutherland said, "They may not be able to fix it, and in that case I'll go down to Brisbane." This was a blow—worse than a dead fish in the face, and General MacArthur almost reeled. He went back in and sat down. For some time, then and in the next day or two, he tried to analyze such behavior. "Brisbane!—Four thousand miles away!—Dick must be sick.—What's wrong with him, Doc?—Is he off his rocker?— The Luzon campaign right in front of him. A pinnacle for his career—and he goes off to Brisbane." He was sure that was where Sutherland would go—and he did, returning just in time for the ceremonial entry into Manila. I learned long after, that General Sutherland had indeed been ill. He had high blood pressure, very high, of which he told no one.

A day or so later we went to call on General Krueger at his headquarters, several miles southeast of Dagupan. On the way over, the General said, "You know, I want to talk to Walter to see if I can persuade him to go down the plain a little bit faster. I think he feels that every side valley on our east is full of Japanese ready to come storming out. Well, there are plenty of Japanese back there, but they're defending the Cagayan Valley where they hope to make a last big stand, and they are not going to come charging down into the plain with all that we have here."

When we arrived at the Sixth Army headquarters, we went to General Krueger's house rather than to any office. His house was a medium-sized one, typical of those built for managers of factories or mills in tropical areas, with a large screened-in porch. The General and he talked privately, and I nosed around just a bit before going outside to see what the headquarters looked like. In the room fronting on the porch was a large pile of books, paperbacks, fifty or seventy-five of them, not a stack but more like a stack that had been kicked over. All the titles that I could see were mystery and spy stories which, I later gathered from Colonel Hagen, the Sixth Army surgeon, General Krueger really needed as an escape from his responsibility for the lives of all the men fighting under him.

After an hour or so, we returned, and on the way back the General didn't say very much. Once he shook his head and said, "Walter's pretty stubborn. Maybe I'll have to try something else."

The next day he sent me off on an errand back to General McNider's outfit and he asked Larry and Bonner Fellers and, I think, Andres Soriano, his pre-war Philippine friend and personal G2, to go down the valley towards Manila and find him a new advanced headquarters as far forward as they could get. He suggested a sugar *central*, a sugar mill serving a large area, as a possibility. One might now be occupied by one of our regimental command posts. He said if they found a good one, he intended to move right away. I went off on my mission toward the northeast, where the progress inland was still slow, and returned just before Larry and the others came back with their report. They had found something that they thought was ideal—a fairly large sugar *central* which was being used as a regimental headquarters, with the enemy at that time just a couple of miles beyond.

The sugar *central* was called San Miguel and was situated on a rise of ground in a nice grove of trees about twenty miles southeast of Tarlac, a town almost halfway between Dagupan and Manila. We had occupied Tarlac a little earlier, and the General had visited it and looked around hard in hope of finding the place where his father had made his headquarters during the Philippine campaign at the turn of the century. Had there been any indication of its existence, that would have been our headquarters. The General didn't often speak of his father, but when he did, it was with the warmest admiration, pride, and a certain wistfulness, as though he wished that that famous general could see what his son was doing now. Times had changed and methods of warfare had changed, but I think he would have gloried in leading an old-fashioned charge such as his father so gallantly and courageously led up Missionary Ridge during the Civil War—before he was twenty years old.

Two days later General MacArthur moved his advanced headquarters down to the San Miguel sugar *central*. That put us fifty or sixty miles in front of General Krueger. In other words, the advanced general headquarters was fifty or sixty miles forward of the army headquarters. As one can well imagine, it speeded up the campaign towards Manila. General Krueger immediately pushed the front another twenty miles farther south, and from then on there was steady pressure and a heightening of the tempo to take Manila. During those first few days in our new headquarters, I was very busy ignoring the General's cold. He hadn't mentioned it to me, so I pretended I was unaware of it.

The people who ran the sugar *central* must have lived well, for there was a cluster of buildings—a fine one for the headquarters and a number in which to live. The open, tropical buildings with large, screened porches were very nicely finished inside. Whereas in Tacloban I had slept in the room next to the General's, both small dark rooms, here he had a large suite to himself, and Larry and I and Andres Soriano were comfortably situated at the other end of a large bungalow.

The General wished he had acted earlier and moved faster, for we'd given the Japanese time to blow up every single bridge between Dagupan and Manila, a number that amounted to well over two hundred that our combat engineers had to repair or replace. However, General Krueger was a cautious and careful man. Like the General, he was very conscious of the lives of his troops. This caution gave the General great confidence in him, though at times he disagreed and grew impatient when, as in this instance, slow progress prevented the exploitation of certain advances.

From San Miguel the enemy was about 25 miles away to the west, 15 or 20 to the east, a short though increasing distance to the south where Manila lay, now only 60 miles away.

11

MacArthur in a Jeep

"We should have Clark Field by now," the General said. Dinner was over and the other generals had returned to their own quarters. General MacArthur, Larry and I were relaxing on the General's porch, where the air was dry and cool. "We should be announcing the capture," the General continued, "but I can't corroborate it. Walter Krueger says not yet, but I'm not sure his communication with his troops is that good. Tomorrow we'll have a look." He had been busy in his office all day, sparring a bit with the Pentagon.

Clark Field was about twenty-five miles southwest of Tarlac, just beyond Route 3, and was an objective that the General hoped very much to have in our hands by the 26th or 27th of January. It was an excellent field, very important for us in our campaign, and he had promised the Central Pacific Forces that he would give them land-based air support when they attacked Okinawa. Clark Field was to base heavy bombers for that operation.

Larry had been talking to a number of correspondents and was irked with them and with the General, who he thought had interfered a bit with good public relations. I had been out in the jeep all day finding out just where we were in contact with the enemy directly east of San Miguel. This meant probing three or four or more places until I knew the enemy was close, marking them as well as I could on a map and going over it with the General when I returned. Both

118

Larry and I were now glad to relax with the General and talk of unimportant things. Whenever a gecko sounded, the General would always interrupt the talk to count the lizard's regular utterings: *gecko, gecko, gecko,* supposedly telling its age—a year per gecko.

Communication with the combat troops was obviously not immediate, but General MacArthur, as I have indicated, had the feeling that we were on the verge of taking Clark Field. So the next day we drove over to Route 3, the main north/south route in the valley, and went down it. Pretty soon we met a buttoned-up tank coming north. When its commander saw the five stars on our jeep bumper, he pulled in front of us, opened his turret, jumped down, came over and said, "My God, sir, you can't go beyond this point. They're shelling the road down there and hitting this part too." A half mile down we could see shell puffs, clouds of cement dust, and chunks of cement and soil sailing through the air. The General asked him a few questions, ending with, "Thank you, Major, but I think I'll just go down and have a look." And we did.

The barrage continued on the road until we were two or three hundred feet away, and I couldn't believe that he wasn't going to turn back. However, at that point the shelling suddenly stopped, and we went through and on for several more miles. But we didn't leave Route 3 and soon turned north—past the barrage area, still quiet, and on to San Miguel.

The next day, information from the Sixth Army still reported Clark Field in enemy hands, but we heard strong rumors that we had taken it. Reports through the Army chain of command could well be a day slow, and since we had probably reached a corner of the field, the General, with his urgent feeling about its capture, announced in a communiqué that it was in our hands. So we went down the same day to corroborate the communiqué, as it were. This was about the 26th of January. At that time the 40th Division was coming at Clark Field from the north and the west, and the

37th was trying to take it from the east. However, the Japanese, anxious to keep this area, fought tenaciously with frequent counterattacks in force, and we had not taken Clark Field that day. So the next day we went farther down Route 3 and then turned west to approach it near its southeastern edge. There were no road signs, there was no front; there were groups, whether tanks, infantry, or artillery, but nothing like a continuous front. And it was very difficult to know just where the fighting was. We drove up a little dirt road and saw one soldier crawling along—a point man, I think— and when we asked him where the enemy was, he said he wasn't sure. He thought there were enemy troops just ahead of him, but he'd heard some firing over there to the left. So we went over the the left and soon found we were on a narrow trail, just wide enough for a jeep, going through a cane field. The General was getting more and more eager to have a look at Clark Field. Ahead of us there was a little hill on the left, and we could certainly hear firing, not only machine gun, but what sounded like a 105-millimeter cannon. The cane was higher than the jeep, so we could only see out now and then where the cane had been blown down or trampled. The General said, "Look for a wire. That'll take us to an observation post or a command post." And just after he said this, there was a wire lying along the edge of the trail. He saw it when we did and told the driver to follow it. Little as I knew about wires, it looked awfully thin for an American signal wire, so I said to the General, "I don't think that's our wire. It might take us to a Japanese O.P. [observation post]." He looked at me as though to say, "What's the matter? Are you worried?," and said to the driver, "Follow it."

And we followed it, with the noise getting louder and louder until suddenly we shot out of the cane field, into the open—between the lines!

Fifty or sixty yards on our right was a battery of 105-millimeter cannon firing point-blank at three Japanese machine-gun emplacements, about an equal distance to our left, but fortunately about thirty feet above us on the hill. The

Signal Corps, U.S. Army

Have we taken Clark Field? January 27, 1945.

Yes! We have taken Clark Field!

Signal Corps, U.S. Army

Japanese were pouring a heavy stream of fire at the cannons. We were literally under fire from both sides. Our driver, a resolute Swede, would have kept going right ahead, but the General shouted, "Back up, back up!" And we backed up into that canebrake very fast, then turned around. The wire obviously had been going to a Japanese post of some kind, so I jumped out and cut it.

I've forgotten how we got home, but we didn't see Clark Field that day, though we heard that evening that the 37th Division was on it. The next day we set out in two jeeps to find it, hoping to set foot on it. We found a better road, and we certainly went through a fair amount of what might be called no-man's land, but reached a point where we could see the field, see the hangars, see the damage, and see and hear some fighting still going on at the far end. This relieved the General, but the main thing he said was: "We kept our commitment."

We did go back a few days later to look at it in detail and get some estimate of how long it would take to have planes taking off. While there was a fair amount of destruction of hangars and planes and parts of the runways, there was a tremendous amount of equipment, supplies, aircraft engines, and so forth, that were captured with the field. He gave his benediction: "George's bombers will be taking off from here in a few days now."

At San Miguel, he certainly was in some ways a restless man. Manila was close; there was fighting all around us— east, west, south, and northeast. He was anxious to get a feel of it all first-hand. It still irked him to get a report from company, to regiment, to division, to corps, to army, to him, for he felt it was apt to be diluted and stale. We went forward at least every other day. Sometimes he would stop at division headquarters and ask the division general to join him. Sometimes he would go directly to the front with both Larry and me or one of us, in the jeep.

Once when he stopped at division headquarters, he was angered. The division had been told that he was coming;

there was great orderliness, much standing at attention in front of tents, as though for an inspection in the United States. The officers seemed immaculate, something hard to maintain in that dusty country, and the aura was certainly one of "the inspection is the thing." He told the commanding general quietly but with feeling that his division was in action, and while spit and polish was very useful between wars or between campaigns, this was no time for it.

The fighting was so often near a road that we would drive forward till we heard, saw, or smelled it; then he would get out and walk until we found somebody who could tell us what the General wanted to know. That was: the tenacity of the enemy, his apparent strength, his firing power, and of course, ours; what our immediate objective was and where we hoped to be in the next two or three days. The General always stood up to talk and seemed unmindful of rifle fire.

On one occasion in particular he thought the going was precarious in a section of our eastern "front" and decided to go there to see for himself and provide rallying support by his presence. We drove as close as we could get and then got out and walked. We went through a virtual graveyard of Japanese soldiers—buried, partially buried, recently killed. As we approached the very busy part of that combat sector, there was a leg and a boot sticking out of the ground, the toes pointing the way, as it were. This macabre signpost horrified me, and I suddenly thought of the rest of him. Not far beyond this we reached a large tree. There was a young colonel crouching in the grass below it and all about were soldiers on their bellies behind logs or rocks or inching forward and shooting. The General and I were alone at this point; the driver of course had stayed with the jeep. When the colonel saw the General he stood up with a look of incredulity on his face. The General hardly needed to introduce himself, the colonel did, and the General started asking questions.

"You must have had hard going crossing that field back there."

"Yes sir, we had a number of casualties too. That's why I came up."

"What's ahead in the woods?"

"Several platoons at least; but we think they are bringing up more. The firing increases."

The General looked across and said, "Rifle fire, what else?"

"That machine gun and two others—no artillery."

At that moment "that machine gun" in the woods sixty yards in front of us was picking leaves off the tree above us. Leaves and twigs were almost raining down on us. Had the gunner lowered his sights it would have been us, not the leaves and twigs.

"What's your plan of action?"

"I have half a platoon over on the right where the wood comes this way; BAR [Browning Automatic Rifle] men and a machine gun. I think this contact is narrow and they should be able to outflank them."

"Good. How are the men?"

"Hard fighters, sir, but it's been rough."

General MacArthur and the colonel talked further, but my mind wandered to that machine gun in front of us. Why didn't we have one? Then I saw an aid man on his belly dragging a wounded man back. He had a very bloody shoulder. Then another obviously in shock, his neck badly hit. Then I saw one of ours dead. Why didn't the General crouch so the colonel and I could do the same? Why, I couldn't tell. He was obviously very much interested in his conversation with the colonel. How did the colonel feel about standing?

We stood there five or ten minutes. The machine gun stopped for a while—out of ammunition, or had the gunner been hit? Then it started again, but found another target.

Finally we walked back. The colonel walked with us, but not very far. As we continued toward the jeep he dropped closer to the ground as he worked his way back to that little strongpoint.

On our way to the jeep we met the first of some troops

coming up to strengthen our position. The General stopped
and talked a moment with a few and greeted (not saluted)
others. The look on their faces ranged from the cynical or
deadpan to the popeyed.

The trip back was quiet. Somehow on this trip, this particular trip, I thought the General wanted not only to encourage, but also to be kept aware through personal observation and participation in the awfulness of war. The
expedition certainly helped stoke the fires that kept him
thinking, "How can I save our lives? How can we take our
objective with the least loss?"

As we came closer to Manila, the number of visits to the
front increased. What the General considered the front was
usually where rifle- and machine-gun fire was going on. At
Clark Field we certainly plopped between the lines and on
one occasion were behind the Japanese. Usually the high
point of such a trip was the nearness of the enemy, a feeling
that at least we were sharing the receiving end, but several
times the high points for me were the conversations.

There were times when something would trigger a train of
thought and the General would express his views on military
matters. At other times he would talk about people and their
qualities, or, as I have said, of strategy. Coming home from a
visit to an active area, he and I were usually alone in the jeep
with the driver. He would turn around. In his seat beside the
driver, he liked to turn around when he talked, so I frequently moved over to the left side of the back seat to make
conversation easier.

Once he came out of a silence and said, "You know, Doc,
it's not so hard to find a good division general." He then went
on to tell me that a good division commanding general could
still relate to his troops, knew many of them, both officers
and men; many more knew him. He could lead in a personal
way, belonging to a group that one could encompass. He
could show concern, sadness; he could weep, and even, on
occasion, exhort. A division commander was a good man,
and in his work, usually a satisfied man; but to find a man

who could command an army was an entirely different proposition. An army commander had to divorce himself from the men of his division or the men of the other divisions, had to work with his staff, relate to them in an entirely different way. His work was more on an intellectual level; he couldn't think of individuals. Emotions or spirit had to be down-played. "No," he said, "it's hard to find such a man." From his wistfulness in describing the former I thought perhaps the division commander's job still held a warm appeal for him.

Another day when we were on our way back from an area just northeast of Manila, he asked me, "What kind of qualities would you like to find in men working with or for you?" The qualities of courage and calmness came to my lips, but the General was at some different level. He said, "I'll tell you," and with emphasis he did, laying out the three most important qualities and the order of their importance. Loyalty came first, very much so—loyalty to his superior, loyalty to the cause that both are fighting for, or working for, loyalty to the people down the line as well as loyalty upwards. He emphasized that unless those below sensed their superior officer's loyalty he would be on quicksand. Next in importance came courage—physical courage, bravery, and moral courage, a courage that applies in peacetime as well as war. And third came intelligence, which he felt was often touted out of proportion. Of course one wanted intelligent people, rather bright people. "But you don't need the brightest ones if that should sacrifice either of the first two qualities." He ended by saying, "There aren't very many situations where extreme brightness is overly important.

The General certainly expressed the loyalty theme towards those who had worked for him, to a high and sometimes blind degree. Those who had been with him on Bataan or on Corregidor or in the Philippines before the war were people he knew and felt he could count on. Some were all he could ask for, but some lacked qualities or abilities he now needed—and might have been replaced by others. He kept them, however, all or most of them. He could count on their loyalty in a personal way, and he stayed loyal to them.

San Miguel was a good, productive, and rather relaxed headquarters. General MacArthur liked it very much in many ways and certainly enjoyed his table there. It was the generals' table and it was much more cheerful than the one at Tacloban. In Tacloban, in the Price house, we were crowded in a very dark room and had the constant air attacks that I have described. At San Miguel, we had a large open room; wherever the officers of the mess had been in the daytime, wherever their duties had taken them, the leisurely hour of dinner in that room was looked forward to and enjoyed. The conversation was varied; it might deal with the European war, sometimes with politics, occasionally a book that somebody had read. A certain amount of business may have been done by people sitting next to each other, but the general tenor of the table was not business. Occasionally there would be a ganging up on somebody whose behavior in one way or another the others had not liked. If it became really heated, the General would say, "Gentlemen, gentlemen," and start the talk off in a positive direction—anywhere.

At this table were the General's immediate staff: General Sutherland, Chief of Staff; General Richard Marshall, Deputy Chief of Staff; General Casey, Chief of Engineers; and General Sverdrup, the deputy Chief of Engineers; General Stivers; General Marquardt; General Willoughby, who usually came to the table with a handkerchief up his sleeve that had some delightful eau de cologne on it, which I envied him. General Chamberlin always joined us when he came up from Leyte. Larry and I made up the rest. The table was not seated according to rank.

We occasionally had visitors such as General Kenney of the Air Force, or Carlos Romulo, but I never remember General Krueger being there or General Eichelberger, his two ranking combat generals. General MacArthur knew all of these people, felt comfortable, was relaxed, had easy conversation with whomever sat next to him. He held forth in general conversation with a natural, easy voice that welcomed anybody joining in. There was no drinking of alcoholic beverages at the table, and I doubt there was much beforehand, but this might not have been entirely voluntary.

While we were based in New Guinea we took up a collection among those officers of GHQ who were interested in trying to get some liquor sent over from the States. I think we each put in $10 or $20, and the shipment arrived in Hollandia after we had gone to Leyte. It stayed there, on the dock, but after we had landed in Lingayen Gulf we thought it might be nice to have what amounted to a modest supply. However, the General controlled the priorities of anything that was to come forward to this advanced headquarters, so he personally had to give permission for the space needed to bring it up. Nobody wanted to ask him. Finally, at the behest of three or four of the generals, it was decided that General Richard Marshall, the Acting Chief of Staff, should do so. Marshall certainly didn't like the job, nor did he feel strongly about the issue, but he agreed to do it. So, after dinner one night, while three or four of the generals were sitting around talking with General MacArthur, General Marshall took a deep breath and started out with a rather general conversation. Finally he led it around to the specific situation that there was a certain amount of liquor on the dock at Hollandia which belonged to us and which we felt we could use, and since it was really very little, and wouldn't weigh very much or take very much room, would the General give us a priority to have it or part of it sent up? It was hardly a strong selling statement.

General MacArthur thought a while and then said, "What are the men drinking?" Several of the officers were glad to assure the General that the men were drinking very good beer, to which I could have added the word "warm." The General after a few moments said, "Well, if the beer is so good for the enlisted men, I should think that it would be good for the officers too." And that was the end of that effort. After the war I met a sergeant who told me about the cache of liquor on the dock at Hollandia and how well he had benefitted financially by selling it to the soldiers.

The campaign of the Luzon plain was drawing to a close. The Japanese had been fought and swept out of it. They had strongpoints in the Zambales mountains to the west, a few lesser strongpoints to the northwest. They still held the Bataan peninsula, and in the large Cagayan Valley to the northeast of us General Yamashita had 200,000 troops. However, his present intent seemed to be to hold that valley and the approaches to it and not come back through the Caraballo Mountains. So our thinking and our planning turned towards Manila.

12

On to Manila

The General wanted to be among the first into Manila. "Doc, I want to get in there early. Three years ago I was driven out of there—made it an open city to save it. I want to be with the first group that enters." So he decided to go in with the First Cavalry, for they, with their flank attack, were to be the first in.

The 37th Division was advancing at a steady but slower pace along Route 3, in the center of the Tarlac plain, which was about fifty miles wide as it approached Manila. The plan had been for the 37th to take and hold the city. The First Cavalry was to penetrate well into the city to relieve Santo Tomas, the large civilian internee camp and nearby Bilibid Prison, where the Japanese held 800 to 1000 Allied prisoners of war. These groups would be in jeopardy of harm by the Japanese, given time.

We got up early on February 5th, but messages from Washington delayed the General, so that when we joined the First Cavalry it was with the main body of the division instead of the spearhead as he had hoped. Larry and I were in the back seat of the jeep. The General as always sat next to the driver. We started working our way forward among the larger vehicles, and were shortly expecting to join the leading tanks and armored trucks. Here Route Five ran along the hilly, dry eastern edge of the valley. There were scattered trees and gullies, dry creek beds and, just before Manila, a wide and deep ravine. There we hit a traffic jam of tanks, half-tracks, trucks, and jeeps; the Japanese had blown up the bridge after our first elements had crossed it.

It was a major obstacle. Either the bridge had to be repaired or a temporary road built to the bottom of the ravine, a bridge thrown across the stream, and a road up the opposite side before we could move forward. The General was distressed and disappointed, for he would have given much to come into Manila with the first troops. We could go no farther forward with the jeep, so he asked me to find someone in authority who might describe the situation. I found a major who, a bit startled at my query, took a look at my insignia, which indicated I was General MacArthur's aide, spoke a few words to a sergeant who was with him, and came over.

"Major, when do you expect to cross this arroyo?"

"I am afraid we don't know, certainly not today, sir."

"No other bridge? No other way around?"

"We have scouts out, but our maps show nothing usable anywhere near us, sir." The General was silent. I knew how deeply unhappy, how let-down he was, but the major couldn't see that.

"Thank you, major," said the General, and then to the driver, "Back to San Miguel." Profoundly disappointed, he was silent until our return, when he went straightway into his office.

The next morning, after a very early start, we caught up with the 37th Infantry Division working its way down Route 3. They were moving slowly for a number of reasons; we joined them below Angeles and, having a rather aggressive driver, we were soon in the vanguard. We were passing through open fields and some sugarcane, bamboo thickets, woods, and the occasional small barrio. We had to stop several times to determine the possible significance of frequent fire-fights a few hundred yards east of the road. These were exchanges of rifle fire with the enemy at relatively close quarters. The first fire-fight to stop us was caused by a small detachment of Japanese holed up in some farm buildings. I doubt any of them escaped. The second was in open fields of knee-high grass, another in a large thicket, and so on. After a five-or ten-minute wait in the first two instances, it was clear they were only isolated pockets, so we proceeded and didn't stop for others.

As we got closer to Manila, where the smoke from the burning buildings and oil dumps was rising high, the road filled up and our movement became very slow. The congestion on our road and the slowing-down of our column was caused by the Filipino people who had come pouring north from Manila, mostly on foot, with now and then a horse and a cart. They filled up the road in front of us and took up the edges on both sides as we came through. Some were moving toward the city but most, and they were women, children, and some men, were coming out. Our pace slowed to five miles an hour.

I thought this was a poor way for an army to go in to take a city, and I remembered the regulations governing the traffic on the military highway between Rawalpindi in India and the Valley of Kashmir when I had been there in 1923. So I said, "General, you know on the military road into Kashmir from the Punjab they had a rule that people in motor vehicles could use the highway from sunrise to sunset and the local population using bullock carts or their own backs could use it from dusk to dawn. Wouldn't that be a good idea? We could give the civilians the road for one part of the day and, with them off the road the rest of the time, we could go in at 30 or 40 miles an hour."

The General looked at me—I wasn't sure how to characterize the look—possibly one with a touch of pity. Then he looked at the people again, then at our trucks just barely moving, and then up ahead at the smoke over the city. After a pause he said, "Don't you see what I see, Doc? Look at the people on the left-hand side of the road here. Nearly all of them are coming *from* Manila. They're frightened, scared—look at their faces. They're running away from something horrible, something for which we share responsibility. Many of them may have seen some of their friends or relatives executed by the Japanese yesterday or even this morning, for *they* must be pretty close to panic now, and look at that smoke and what it means!"

He turned his head a bit. "Look at those on the right-hand side of the road. Most of them are going toward Manila," and most of them were, "and every one of them has something he is pushing or pulling or carrying. See that man pushing the baby carriage? It will be full of food." He went on with increasing emphasis to tell me that that was a food line for Manila, that those people had come out into the country to find food for their families. There was an urgency in his voice, and he underlined that with his forefinger as he said we mustn't stop those frightened people from leaving the city. He was quiet again for a while and then, "No, Doc, it has to be a lot worse. We have to be threatened much more than at present before we put any added burdens on the civilian population. We'll let them move freely, obeying their fears or bringing back food."

So we progressed slowly, four or five miles an hour, at times perhaps up to ten. The fields became spotted with scattered houses and then gave way to clusters of gray brick buildings and then as recognizable streets appeared, narrow but not as narrow as in the Orient, our civilian companions, the Filipinos, seemed to disperse up the side streets, while those fleeing Manila must have used other routes. They quickly disappeared, as though we represented danger rather than safety. This part of the city had not been burned.

The sudden, intoxicating realization that we were in Manila, our goal of the past two and a half years and a major landmark on the way to Tokyo, had to be shelved as we observed not only that none of its people could be seen, but that shooting was going on all around us.

We now had to leave the main body of our troops and find our way to the first place General MacArthur wanted to see: Bilibid Prison, where some eight or nine hundred American and Allied prisoners were kept. (A great many others had been sent to such camps as Cabanatuan and Los Pinos, forty to fifty miles from the city, or across the seas to Manchuria.) Our jeep with one other traveled many streets, took many turns until we passed on our left a large, long, gray building with a few barred windows, far apart, and near its center a large wooden door. This was the back door to Bilibid, which was opened to us not many hours after the first American troops had come in through the front door. We entered a small hall and were soon met by the thinnest man I have ever seen out of bed, Major Warren Wilson, M.C., a doctor from Los Angeles, captured on Bataan three years earlier. Major Wilson, an ophthalmologist, was the senior officer in charge of what now could only be described as a hospital. Thin he was, and tired he looked, but the warmth of his smile and welcome touched both the General and me deeply. He came to attention, saluted, and in a soft, hoarse voice said, "Welcome to Bilibid, sir." The General shook hands with him, obviously moved, and said, "I am glad to be back."

Behind Major Wilson's welcome, expressed for all the prisoners, lay three years of faith and hope, of less and less food to the point of gradual starvation; of the reduction to the eating of grubs, insects, fish guts, to swollen legs and swollen bellies, as starvation, with its scurvy and pellagra, took over; of bleeding from the mouth, slow thinking, extreme loss of weight, and overweening weakness. They had in the past few months begun to die in rapidly increasing numbers.

These men—American, Norwegian, British, and a few other Allies—were sitting by their cots or on them, or lying on them. As the General entered the large rooms that could now only be described as wards, and the men saw him, some knew quickly who he was and what it meant. Some eyes remained vacant, others smiled, many wept, and the sitting tried to stand—many couldn't. Those lying tried to sit up, and most failed. The General shook hands or more often put a hand on a shoulder as he leaned back or forward and caught a man's eyes with his. He greeted them with a quiet and husky voice.

Some spoke: "I never thought I'd see you, sir," said a black-haired American boy standing up straight for half a minute.

"Dear God, dear God," sobbed another sitting on a chair.

"Mr. General, thank you," from a Norwegian, and so on. We went from ward to ward, the General moving among the men until he had greeted most; his smile was warm, his eyes were bright, and he was deeply moved as I heard him murmur again and again, "My boys, my men—it's been so long—so long."

It was time to leave. General MacArthur turned to Major Wilson again, "Arrangements are being made for food, hospitalization, and whatever else these men need?"

"Yes sir, medical care and food are on the way."

"Good—you have done well through these years. Good-bye, and thank you."

We returned to the jeep. The General admitted feeling as emotionally drained as he looked. We had to press on immediately to our next objective, Santo Tomas, where 4,000 civilian internees were held.

These had been liberated by that small detachment of the First Cavalry Division consisting of light tanks and armored vehicles which had crossed the bridge over the ravine before the Japanese blew it up and delayed us for a day. This detachment, without support from the rest of the force halted at the ravine, had continued as planned, reached the encampment, and blown open the main gates. The Japanese there had surrendered without harming the internees whose wild expressions of joy and gratitude to God and their deliverers, we were told, almost undid the cavalrymen.

We drove through quiet walled streets to an open area in front of high walls topped by red tiles. Through large gates guarded by our men, we entered a spacious courtyard surrounded by the wall behind us and big buildings on the other three sides. The courtyard was full of happy, talking people, and more clustered in the windows. This had been a Catholic

Leaving Bilibid Prison with Major Wilson. In the foreground are some of the few Allied prisoners of war who could still stand. The prison was in the Philippines.

university which had been turned into an internee camp for men, women, children, whole families. Mostly Americans, there were also British, French, and Norwegians, but no Spaniards, since Spain had been neutral, and no Germans. Many, including a number of business leaders among them, had known General MacArthur before the war. The welcome was hysterical as he was thoroughly surrounded by happy, shouting, talking, weeping people. He couldn't move. I think this occasion made him happy, but the contrast to Bilibid was unnerving, and after ten minutes or so I thought he gave me a signal to get him out.

We then went behind the buildings to an amazing encampment on the grounds of the university. Here, made of boards, of tin, of palm thatch, were six or seven hundred family dwellings—not shacks, for they were well kept—laid out in streets like an army encampment, though not as straight, and providing bare privacy. There was shade from trees, bamboos and banana plants; there were water and common sanitary facilities. It was a town of children and adults who, in the early days, if they had money, had been allowed to purchase from the Filipino population outside the walls such things as food to supplement their rations and materials to make their lives more comfortable.

During the past six months, however, their fare had rapidly diminished. An increasing number had become ill and weak enough with scurvy and undernourishment to require hospitalization. For all of them, starvation like that at Bilibid was probably two or three months off. We visited many of those huts, spoke with women, children, and men, American and otherwise. They were eager to talk or just to look at or to touch the General, whom they saw as the symbol and the force that had not only freed, but saved them.

One could see that the General was getting restless and uneasy, and at the end of another hour he said, "This has been a bit too emotional for me. I want to get out and I want to go forward until I am stopped by fire,"—and after a slight hesitation—"and I don't mean sniper fire."

This we did. We got into our jeep again—the General,
Andres Soriano, who joined us at Santo Tomas, Larry and I.
I wondered where "forward" was. It could be any direction
other than due north. The General chose south and we were
off, followed by a jeep-load of BAR men (soldiers carrying
Browning automatic rifles). To the General this was familiar
territory, and he led us toward the Pasig River, which our
forces had not yet crossed. As a matter of fact, we only had
spotty occupation of the north side of the river. We saw no
civilians, but we did meet a few light tanks and armored cars.

Turning a corner on a broad street, we encountered a
stationary open truck full of Japanese soldiers—some with
guns in their hands standing up leaning over the sides,
others sitting, all dead. Grotesque as it was, it made one think
of a ghastly *tableau vivant.* As we continued, we saw no other
wheeled vehicles, but passed up a street with our soldiers
going in the same direction along the walls on either side,
single file about ten yards apart, walking stooped and watching as though they expected to meet Japanese at any moment. We passed them and soon arrived in front of a
tremendous unharmed building between us and the river.
This was the San Miguel Brewery.

Since this was the brewery of Andres Soriano, who had
been talking to our driver and possibly giving directions, I
thought perhaps our arrival there was no coincidence. Soriano jumped out of the jeep and waved at the building.
Luckily it was his workers, not Japanese, who came out with a
warm and joyous welcome, about six or eight of them from
the higher echelons of his staff. The brewery, apparently
inactive, was in good condition, and a celebratory toast by us
all was indicated as required, there in the middle of the
street, with a sip, quaff, or glass of San Miguel beer. The
General, impatient to go on, touched a glass to his lips but
didn't drink.

He asked Soriano to ask his staff what lay ahead. They said
that the Japanese still occupied this part of the city. In spite
of this news, six of us—the General, Andres Soriano, Larry

The General greets an old friend at Santo Tomas, Manila.

and I, and two BAR men—started off on foot, more or less parallel with the river. After three or four minutes of walking rather slowly along in the middle of the street, I began to hear the sound of bullets, bullets coming in our direction. They came irregularly—sniper fire. I carried a light gun, a carbine, and held it at the ready; but I couldn't locate any shooters on rooflines, in top story windows, or anywhere else. The bullets that passed were close, not many feet away, and those that hit the pavement were within ten or fifteen feet. When you can't do anything else you count those that missed you. I had counted between 25 and 30 bullets when, as we were passing a large building on our left, a soldier came out of a doorway, saluted in amazement, and said the next cross-street about 30 yards away was covered by Japanese machine-gun fire from the river. While the General was asking him a few questions, there was a burst of machine-gun fire in front of us to prove his statement. I tried not to look at the General as I prayed that the burst was the message that would send us back. The General decided it was, that he had seen and felt enough; and so we walked back to our jeeps and then started back towards Santo Tomas and San Miguel.

13

Return to Bataan

Before dinner on February 15, the General said, "Doc, tomorrow we will be going down to Bataan." It was different from his other statements of plans—it came from deep down—and from his look one knew not to talk again right away. That meant that the next morning we would get up several hours earlier than usual and set off in a jeep in a southwesterly direction until we could taste fighting, see its awful cost in the dead of both sides, get the full tactical picture while being well-exposed to fire, visit with the wounded, and perhaps get hit ourselves. Bataan peninsula, the scene of the Death March of American captives in 1942 when Japan took the Philippines, would be our destination.

I knew that the 151st Regimental Combat Team had landed at Mariveles (near the tip of Bataan) that day, and that part of it was to work its way up the east coast of the peninsula. I also knew that the 503rd Parachute Regiment was making a drop on Corregidor the following day, and the 38th Division had just fought its way over the Zigzag Pass from the head of Subic Bay and, finally, that the 1st Infantry of the Sixth Division was starting down the east coast of Bataan peninsula. Knowing all that, I could sense where he wanted to be: in the middle of it. For some reason, hard to assess now, I too liked going forward and was up at 4:30 on the 16th with a sense of eagerness. After an early breakfast

144

we were off, the General, Larry and I, followed by a jeep-load of correspondents who sensed something was up.

I am sure I can make this trip come to life best by quoting from a letter I wrote to Mrs. MacArthur the following day:

We got up at quarter to five, started off long before dawn, and reached San Fernando about first light. Picked up General Edelman who was the G3 of the Sixth Army, and a jeep-load of BAR men . . . . Then southwest along the road that you must know well in your mind's eye—the road along which the Americans retreated towards Bataan and along which as captives they later made their March of Death. The General was lost in thought and, I am sure, memories, as we drove along this good road past the fish farms and across the rice fields of the Pampangas and towards the Zambales Mountains, just catching the first sun. You could see the stream of peasants bringing their barnyard produce, vegetables and so forth, to market, handsome women, gracefully erect as they carried baskets on their heads, men struggling along at a dogtrot with heavier things hanging from poles. But you can't see the evidence of past and present campaigns that we saw as we went along: recent ruins sporadically occurring, a whole block of ashes and twisted corrugated iron roofing—or that destruction which unmistakably was of 1941 and 1942, cleaned up neatly but not rebuilt. There were also the grass-covered ruins that might have been from '98 or defenses against the Chinese sea pirates of old. Through all this we drove, through supply columns coming forward through the dust, the artillery in the fields on either side of us, the engineers repairing bridges, but the General wasn't looking at the foreground. His eyes were far ahead in the broad sweep of the ridges, on the slopes coming down from the Zambales to that rich coastal plain. And backward in time to the fighting that went on there so desperately and against such heavy odds and which, though Bataan was lost, turned the battle for the Pacific.

He lived with his own thoughts and his old comrades in arms until we got to below Pilar. We had passed the first line of defense and were just through the second of the 1942 campaign. The General began pointing to hidden villages on the slopes of Santa Rosa and he would say, "The Japanese will be collecting up there," or "They will be regrouping over there." We came by our regimental and our present command posts and we arrived at our most forward patrol and there got out to view the effects of a Japanese Banzai attack which had occurred just a few hours earlier. Twenty or thirty dead Japanese sprawled about brought the General up to the present with a shock. Here General Edelman and General Hall, who had joined us, asked him to turn back. None of our men had been forward of this point. The General said, "No, this is easing an ache that my heart has carried for three years. I'm going forward. I'll lead by personal patrol," and he did. Six miles farther into enemy-held territory we went, a little cavalcade of jeeps, down that old stone military road, jungle pressing in on both sides, overhanging banks, prepared positions, tunnels, spider holes, breastworks, by an ammunition dump, until finally a few miles above Cabcaban, we were stopped by a bombed-out bridge. Another few miles and we might see Corregidor, on which our troops were just then landing. But no way across the stream, fortunately. So rather reluctantly, we came back. It did his heart good to see the Japanese demoralized and disturbed to the point of letting us enter their territory that way without stopping us, for there must have been enough of them around to do that.

What I didn't tell Mrs. MacArthur was this, which fills in some of the reined-in sentences:

Pilar was twenty or thirty miles down the east coast of Bataan and about twenty-five miles from Mariveles near its tip. We had picked up several jeep-loads of officers and correspondents at the divisional headquarters. General Hall, Commanding General of the 38th Division, had joined Larry Lehrbas and me in the back seat of the General's jeep. As we left the divisional headquarters, there were eight other jeeps in our convoy, carrying BAR men and officers from the 6th Army headquarters and an overflowing jeep-load of correspondents and photographers, including my friend Carl Mydans who, with his wife Shelley, had been among a shipload of internees from Santo Tomas who had been exchanged some months earlier. We were soon on a cobblestone road, the Death March road, a little in from the coast. We began to see recently killed enemy, two's, three's, a group of ten, along the road. The country, at first open farming country, became rougher and more wooded. Not far below Pilar was dense jungle. While the country was still intermittently open we came on that forward position. The Japanese had really just been repulsed within the half-hour and the survivors had retreated into the woods towards the west, possibly to regroup and attack again. We had also sustained casualties; ponchos covered the bodies of three of our men, jeeps, a command car, and other materiel were still burning, and the captain and his men looked as one would have expected them to look—solemn, wary and weary. I certainly felt deeply the sternness and the sadness of this handful of troops and the grimness associated with all of the dead, and I was sure this would drive the General forward. The captain thought the enemy was in front of us in relative force, and General Edelman and General Hall earnestly urged the General to go no farther. They said the enemy was in considerable strength down the road and across the road.

The General listened silently, then looked up toward the mountains, then looked back the road we had come. Then, hearing there were two scouts a short distance ahead, he turned to the generals and said with deepest feeling, "You can't stop me here! We'll go on. This is my personal patrol." So we got into our jeeps and headed south again. The country continued rather open, fields, trees, large bushes and rocks, and one could glimpse the gentle slopes of that long-extinct volcano, now completely forest-covered, that was over on our right.

About a half mile down the road we did come upon the two scouts progressing carefully along the depression on either side of the road. We stopped again and talked with them. They thought they had heard some Japanese up ahead but weren't sure. "You are the forward point? None of our men ahead of you?" said the General.

"None of our men ahead of here, sir! No sir."

"Larry, Doc, get your carbines unlimbered," and his eyes almost flashed. So we started forward again, reduced to six jeeps by now, General Hall still with Larry and me in the back seat, and three riflemen in the jeep behind us, followed by four jeep-loads of BAR men and generals, colonels, correspondents, and photographers. Soon we were into the dark jungle. This jungle deserves description. The cobblestone road, mossy and slippery in places, had a ditch on either side. The trees and bushes and the climbing and the hanging vines were dense; no flowers, no sun, a wall of growth so thick we could see only a few feet into it. As the road cut through ridges, steep banks overhung us and stopped my thinking beyond the word, *ambush*.

After fifteen or twenty minutes of bumping along at twelve or fifteen miles an hour, we suddenly came into an opening—about an acre of grass and stones—in the jungle. To the left a fire was burning, and over it a pot was steaming but I didn't look there long, for directly in front of us across the clearing I found I was looking up the barrel of a Japanese machine gun. I thought this must be the end of all roads for me, but nothing happened. The Japanese must have left in a hurry on hearing us approach. I found a good pair of field glasses near the fire, which was cooking rice, and that perhaps told the story.

We soon continued on from this spot, with banks rising high on either side and very few open spaces. We passed a small Japanese munitions dump and two of our parachute bombs lying on their sides nearby, another campsite, and then the jungle became less dense until we came to another fair-sized opening and a stream. It was a mile or so before that that we heard over a walkie-talkie that a hundred or more Japanese had come across from the Manila side of the Bay and had landed behind us. I thought, how far behind? How long would it take them to reach us, and which way should we go? Into the jungle toward the mountains, or toward the Bay? However, the General said he didn't think we need be concerned about them: "Just a group of frightened and demoralized soldiers retreating from Manila and coming across to head for the hills to join their comrades." Sure enough, there was no sign of them on the way back.

The stream posed a problem. By now one suspected that

the General was hoping to take his patrol down to meet our forces coming north. Such a meeting was beginning to worry me more than the Japanese. He had said we might possibly watch the parachute landing on Corregidor, but the stream was deep, the bridge was blown, and we could find no place to ford. We were still well short of any spot from which we could see Corregidor and probably eight or ten miles from the task force coming north from Mariveles.

About then I noticed a P-38 passing overhead at an altitude of six or eight thousand feet and thought how good it was to see one of our planes and not a Japanese Zero. However, a few minutes later it came back over us at about fifteen hundred feet, and this had an ominous significance. I waved hard at it in the short time that one could wave at a fighter plane passing over. "General, that may be one of ours, but I bet he thinks we're the enemy. Nobody knows we're here." He didn't say anything, and then I heard the plane returning. This time low and sickeningly close, to the ears of one who has been strafed. I yelled to the General to get behind the jeep engine, since there was no other place to go, and I started waving at the plane like mad as it came in sight. It—he—was only a few hundred feet up and he was aimed right at us, but he didn't pull the trigger and he didn't come back. I found a log on which I very much needed to sit. But not the General. He wandered around a bit with his hands in his pockets, distressed at our not being able to go farther and, I thought, possibly wondering why we weren't going to build a new bridge. I was thanking God and the Japanese for destroying that bridge.

With the southern task force still eight or ten or possibly twelve miles away, there wasn't much point in trying to continue our sortie on foot. In due course, and it seemed like due course, we started back—back past our fallen bombs, back past the Japanese munitions dump and its campsite, back past the machine-gun emplacement (where we got out to take a better look), back past the area where the hundred Japanese from Manila had landed, and finally back to our forward position. We dropped General Hall and most of the BAR men at the division headquarters and continued on home in the dusk. Our road now ran through the quiet countryside, the fish ponds, and the rice paddies, and, finally, Route 3 and so north to San Miguel and a bite of supper. . . . A white tablecloth, silverware—now as unreal as what we had been through—a bed in a good room, and sleep.

Our officers thought that General MacArthur had taken great risks that day. Our G2 said that we had passed thirty enemy tanks and that a thousand soldiers were blocking the road a mile beyond the blown-up bridge. I think he had taken a great risk—but perhaps not as great as it appeared to those of us with less experience. First, he felt the Japanese were pulling in towards the mountainous backbone of Bataan to regroup. It later turned out that they had accumulated four or five thousand troops there. During such a period he felt they would be concentrating on their efforts to unite. That would be their positive action, and during that period they would try to avoid us. They were, in a sense, mentally retreating from us. This would appear to have been true. The banzai attack may well have been a rearguard action; the survivors of that group did in fact retreat up into the mountains. Those who came across the Bay apparently went the same way.

That evening he relived with relish the patrol on which he had taken us, and summed up the tactical situation with, "I was sure the enemy would be heading for the hills—to those places I pointed out to you. That's what I would have done, and changed to guerrilla warfare. Now I'm afraid we shall have to roust them out."

As he dwelt on our nearness to the Japanese at their campsite and elsewhere, he said, "Doc, it's been a long time since I led a patrol into no-man's land. Makes you tingle a bit, doesn't it?" Then his words were followed by a faraway look, and I was sure he wished we might have met some Japanese soldiers a bit slow on the draw or whose first shots had been wild.

This was a deeply emotional time for the General. Probably more than his return to the Philippines, this return to Bataan was the real cleansing of the old defeat, of the ignominy and the starvation and death of his earlier troops. He had said three times that day, "You don't know what a leaden load this lifts from my heart."

14

Testing the Enemy

Douglas MacArthur enjoyed going forward, forward to where active fighting was in progress. On mornings when we would start off for some sector of the front in the Philippines or when we were getting ready to go ashore during a landing, his spirits were up, he was calm and he looked calm, but his gait or his eyes or his voice, or perhaps all three, packed a little extra zing. As I got to know him I recognized this as an indication that he was happy. I had asked him on a number of occasions why he, the Commander-in-Chief of the theater, should go forward quite so much and quite so far—should expose himself the way he had. His usual answer was, "Doc, I want my generals forward, and I certainly don't want to order them, so I go forward too."

He had a deep and unhappy feeling about the way World War I had been fought. He thought it entirely wrong that the higher-ranking officers sat either far behind the lines or deep below the ground, and from that vantage directed the lieutenants or the non-commissioned officers to lead the men in a charge. He said, "A map doesn't tell you everything. It doesn't show you a little hillock or a broad stump or a shallow depression, all of which could protect men using automatic weapons." He said, "Under fire and in a long battle, forests change and the very ground changes." He felt the officers should know all of these details as they ordered their men to take an area, and, to know that, they had to be there. "Besides, it does help morale, you know, when they see a major or a colonel or a general with them. Something happens to the men."

He referred only once to the time during World War I when he led the Rainbow Division personally in an advance that penetrated deep into the German lines, many miles in, and changed the course of a major battle. This was a penetration of a couple of days in which their casualties, though heavy, were apparently only one-fifth of the casualties of the divisions that had been nibbling at that same front over the previous two or three months without any progress.

General MacArthur knew that he had generals who did go forward. There were, among others, General Patrick, who was killed in action at the very front; General Mudge, who, going forward with his point man, was hit by a grenade and almost killed; General Chase, who went ashore with the first wave in the Admiralties. But he wanted to be sure that all of them saw the action. When he took a general forward as he visited a particular sector of the front, he was aware of that general—he was aware of how much he knew about the disposition of his troops, and he was very much aware of how he reacted to being forward under rifle or machine-gun fire. Several were relieved following such visits and sent back to other jobs. But I felt there was more than this, important as it was, to explain some of his behavior at the front.

After landing in the third wave in the Admiralties, why had he gone out in front of all our men, in front of our machine guns, and walked up and down the Momotu airstrip, when he and we knew the Japanese were on the other side of it? Why at the very front on a sector northeast of Manila had he stood under a tree talking with a colonel when all the men were lying on their bellies behind boulders or logs shooting into the woods where the enemy was? Here he and the colonel and a reluctant I were the only ones standing under that tree as an enemy machine gun kept plucking the leaves above. When that colonel left us a little while later, after we had walked back a way, he had had to inch his way forward on his belly to get back to his position.

Why had he calmly walked down the street in Manila when I counted between 25 and 30 sniper bullets aimed at us in the course of one or two blocks? Why, after we had climbed to the top of an apartment building on Rizal Boulevard to see the lay of the land and the action from one of our observation posts, did he stand in the window in full view looking out while the sergeant who manned the post urged, "General, step back, they'll be shooting here." The Japanese did, a number of bullets coming through the window seconds after he stepped behind the wall. Why did he face the muzzles of two machine guns from the Presidente's office in Malacanan and look right at the two Japanese gunners, who perhaps couldn't believe what they saw until he suddenly left the room and they began pulling their triggers? Why did he do these and many, many other acts of unwarranted exposure, almost tauntingly?

One evening when we were at San Miguel getting ready to move our headquarters in to Manila, I asked him. I knew him well enough by then to probe, to make him go farther in his answers, and I said, "You have always told me that you go forward so that your generals will go forward, and I know that argument. It certainly holds water for your going forward, but that doesn't explain those actions where you're almost taunting the enemy. Standing in that window at that O.P. day before yesterday, I wondered whether you were saying, 'Go ahead and shoot.' " I mentioned four or five of the other episodes that I just referred to. I was determined to get a better, fuller answer this time.

He sensed that, smiled and seemed to think a while, possibly arranging his reasons, and then he said, "Doc, there are different reasons, some hard to explain. Perhaps I am not quite sure myself, but first let me say that all those risks

Roger Egeberg

This picture was taken seconds before bullets came through this observation post in an apartment building high above Rizal Avenue in Manila.

are not as great as you may think they are. Don't forget I had a lot of combat experience in World War I—certainly more than any of our present general officers—and as you live through such experiences you learn things. You learn to see things that are dangerous or that are reassuring, and you get a sense of timing."

He referred to the Momotu strip, saying that he knew that we were probably within a hundred yards of the enemy. He didn't know how many, but thought it was a fair number. On the other hand, he was sure they were collecting themselves, gathering reserves from farther back, and getting ready for a counterattack, a banzai charge. While they were doing that, he said they would not shoot, they would lie low. He had discussed this with General Chase who agreed. The enemy did make the banzai charge, and were repulsed, early that evening.

With respect to snipers, he said most of them were not sharpshooters, and he could tell that. Probably not even good shots, they were scared and shot long before they should, when we were almost out of their range. He warmed up: "With respect to those two Japanese machine-gunners across the Pasig from the Malacanan Palace, I was pretty well worked up at that point, reminiscing about the Presidente (Quezon), and perhaps I thought I could stare them down. Then I saw some movements that made me realize they were getting ready to fire. They said something to each other, and we left that room in a hurry, and none too soon.

"Possibly when you have seen as much action and had as much exposure as I have and you haven't been hit, possibly you get the idea you are not going to be hit. I have wondered whether I might have fallen into thinking that I had a job to finish and that I would be allowed to do so. But I don't think so. I enjoy being in action, Doc, I enjoy it. I like to go forward. Sharing the risks that the men are taking does something for me. I think I get strength from it. On one or two occasions perhaps I was testing my timing, but on the whole, I like to think that being relaxed under fire can affect the action and the morale of a whole company."

He became silent, and withdrawn from me, possibly thinking of experiences of which I was unaware. I didn't see any point in asking him whether the term "Dugout Doug," which the Bataan soldiers had given him when he was on Corregidor, in what they thought was safety, had bothered him and egged him on. It was so patently wrong that he didn't need to disprove it further.

I could understand this latter part of the argument through my own reactions. When I was well back from danger, I adapted to a civilian life-pattern. My thoughts were a civilian's thoughts. But when I was intermittently forward in action, alternating with relative comfort and safety, and when I experienced some of what the men in combat had to go through, I felt a desire and almost a need to join with them in their dangers—to take perhaps a little more risk than if I were in a kill-or-be-killed affair extending for a week or more. Possibly there was a sense of guilt over my more fortunate status, but there is no doubt that I also liked going forward. I liked the anticipation of it; I slept well the night before. I did not, however, in any way like the *undue* exposure.

Perhaps these feelings were pointed up by the General on our last evening at the headquarters at the San Miguel Sugar *Central*. It was after the end of the Philippine campaign. He had received a copy of his press release about our reestablishment of the Commonwealth Government in the City of Manila and had just reread it. If he was thinking of certain actions in the campaign, he didn't speak of them. He looked relaxed and content. I think he was smoking a cigar—a rare occurrence. He said, "Doc, you've been through a whole campaign, a fairly rugged campaign, and you have seen much of it. We've been in a number of tough spots when they were at their hottest. We went to the fronts where the fighting was active. We shared with the men." He was silent for a while. "Yes, we've been there—we've been there." He then wrote across the top of the paper he was reading:

To "Doc" with affectionate remembrances of our campaign association.

MacArthur

Luzon, 1945

and gave it to me.

I think General MacArthur was a happy warrior—happier in action than planning it. He fulfilled some inner need or compulsion in taking the risks that the fighting men took.

15

Manila

Once it was secure, Manila began returning to relatively normal living. The Japanese had aimed to destroy primarily the bridges and public buildings; the post office and its contents had burned for days and appeared gutted; the historic old walled city had been demolished as the Japanese defended it to the end. But most office buildings remained, and the Army engineers had retained a pontoon bridge from the combat days and were building Bailey bridges across the Pasig River.

General MacArthur now quickly made arrangements to bring Mrs. MacArthur and the rest of the household up from Brisbane. It had been many months since he had last seen his wife, months and weeks and days that he frequently counted out loud to me. Now, with a definite time schedule, he began to count forward. "Jean will be here in just over two weeks," he said in a satisfied way. No guesswork, no delays— "She'll be here."

The house to which he brought his family was Casa Blanca, a large white house a few miles east of his headquarters. It had thirteen or fourteen rooms. To the side and behind it lay three bungalows of varied sizes. The largest housed the guard detail. Dusty Rhoades, Larry Lehrbas, Major Graham, and I had the middle one, which included a guest room for the higher-ranking military visitors. Between these two structures, Andres Soriano lived in a smaller

160

The Malinta tunnel on Corregidor Island. The General has a look
at the end of the war. March 2, 1945.

The General greets Admiral Nimitz on his arrival at Nichols Field, Manila. May 5, 1945.

cottage in a style that was a compromise between what the Army furnished and his accustomed peacetime manner. Of the Spanish aristocracy, he was also one of the richest men in the Philippines; he had courage but no taste for menial labor, which in his establishment was entirely taken care of by a cook, waiter, scullery man, and outdoor handyman. I was amused one day watching him train his new valet. Among other duties, Soriano showed him how to wind his pocket watch.

By the time Mrs. MacArthur and the household arrived on a freighter in March 1945, the General had been in the field about five months. He had directed and actively participated in the two victorious campaigns of Leyte and Luzon. Now he was looking forward very much to the companionship he had missed.

Reunited with his family, he was relaxed and happy in a different manner from that of his campaign days. He settled down to a schedule. Up at seven in the morning, he would breakfast and then work at home until he went to the office about nine-thirty. He returned for lunch about quarter to two; afterwards, he undressed and went to bed for a good nap, then returned to the office at four and came home again at seven-thirty. Maybe four times a week a movie was shown in the basement; all of us in the Casa Blanca compound were welcome to attend, so that there were usually ten or twelve in the room, which had several rows of seats, General and Mrs. MacArthur customarily sitting alone in the front row.

The General was discerning in his choice of movies. He had favorite actors and actresses and directors. He refused to see war films. One day after he had been offered one, he said, "Doc, I just don't want to see a war movie. I know enough to see too many glaring errors. Dare say you don't relish a hospital movie, do you?"

His headquarters were in the City Hall, a massive building which the enemy, despite their efforts to destroy it, had only dented in one corner. Our engineers had quickly readied the major part for occupancy. The General had what may have been the mayor's comfortable suite in the southeast corner.

Larry Lehrbas or I, or sometimes both together, would accompany the General to and from work, usually in a jeep, for the first month or two. On one occasion we encountered a memorable traffic jam.

Army trucks and cars, bullock carts, horse-drawn vehicles, and pedestrians had all converged on one corner where a poor M.P. (one of ours) was trying to bring some order out of veritable chaos. We came to a dead stop. Thinking the M.P had recognized us, I waited for him to help us through, but instead he cleared the traffic in another direction. The General watched, at first the traffic about us, then the M.P., who was struggling rather unsuccessfully. After what must have been several minutes, he said, "Doc, why don't you go over and see if you can't get that M.P. to let us through." No impatience in his voice or his manner, just a suggestion that we would like to be on our way and that was the man who could help us.

Our GHQ was now planning the landings on Kyushu, the great southern island of Japan. Some sections were already working on the invasion of Honshu, the main island, where Tokyo and the large industrial cities were. The Navy would be heavily involved and at one point Admiral Nimitz came out with some of his staff to discuss their cooperative efforts. We were beginning to get official visitors from the United States, including a number from Congress.

Manila was the first big city that many of our soldiers had seen for a year or more; so when they could do so they would come to visit it, tending to wander around looking mildly disappointed, like the tourists who come to Hollywood. These visits had certain consequences.

In the Army, venereal disease is an enemy to be classed with those who carry guns. It can cause casualties, take men out of action just as well as a bullet and sometimes more frequently, so that a rising venereal disease rate of a company or a regiment or an army becomes a red flag to any medical bull out of a higher headquarters. Our venereal disease rate in Australia had reached a peak high enough to gain critical attention in the Pentagon on the Potomac. In New Guinea, where the rate was the lowest ever, we should have had medals had the authorities used any system of rewards for such a state; but there they probably knew there were no women near the troops.

When we came to the Philippines, however, it was different again. Our V.D. rate didn't rise much among the troops stationed out in the provinces, small towns, and villages, but it started to climb in the big city of Manila. The Filipinos are an attractive people; most of our troops were happy just to enjoy the companionship of a Philippine family after years of jungle fighting. There were, however, always the lustier ones who wanted the company of women for less social, more specialized purposes. Even innocents could be snared, for the Manila pimp was often an engaging nine- or ten-year-old boy who sidled up, grabbed a finger, and said, "Want pom-pom? Want fun? I take you my big sister, she clean." All true but the last statement.

So V.D. rose and rose; and Manila, in spite of its devastation, managed to accommodate the soldiers on this front as well as with trinkets, beer, impromptu dance halls, and so forth. And the news of the venereal disease rate swelled all the way to the Pentagon. After a little warning correspondence two outstanding specialists in this field, epidemiologists, university professors, Dr. Earle Moore and Dr. Thomas Sternberg, came to our theater. Our statistics led them right to Manila and the statistics were bad, bad enough so they felt the only way to slow V.D. down was to put Manila out of bounds to troops. That would mean that none of our soldiers outside Manila could visit it.

Drs. Moore and Sternberg didn't have much luck with their recommendations through the usual channels. They were even dealing with the wrong headquarters for gaining the authority they needed; so more or less in desperation, they asked me if I could help them by calling this problem to the attention of General MacArthur. Since putting Manila out of bounds offered a solution, I agreed to talk to the General. The following morning as we were driving to the office I said, "General, you remember what a very low rate of V.D. we had in New Guinea, in Milne Bay?" He didn't answer, so I dove in: "Well, we are making up for that now; we have a lot of V.D. here. The rate is the highest we've had since we left Australia and is going up. The Surgeon General's office sent over Dr. Moore and Dr. Sternberg, two of their top men in that field, to find out what's wrong, and they have been studying the situation for a week. They think the only thing we can do to reduce it is to cut down the soldiers' opportunities in Manila.'"

"What?"

"Yes. There isn't very much V.D. in those troops that are stationed far away from Manila. It's among those stationed in Manila or who come here when they have a day or two of furlough. You know, all those engaging kids who want you to have pom-pom with their big sister?" I was talking fast. "Well, both syphilis and gonorrhea are way up. Doctors Moore and Sternberg haven't been able to get to you, but they hope you'll see fit to declare Manila out of bounds to our troops."

The General seemed astonished and shot out, "Declare Manila out of bounds to our troops? Why, Doc, do you know what you're asking me to do? You're asking me to tell the soldiers—grown men—who have fought their way through the jungles of New Guinea and through the mud of Leyte and who have braved the Japanese fire on the landings—to stay out of the first city they have seen where they can have any fun, where they can go and perhaps have a drink or two, maybe dance a bit, buy some trinkets, see civilian life?"

He paused, then, "Besides that, you're asking me to cut off one of the main sources of money for the people of Manila, selling things, having restaurants, giving our men relaxation when they're off duty. No, Doc, that's an insult to the soldiers and hard on the disrupted economy of this war-torn city."

Warmed up, he continued, asserting that most of our men were more anxious to see a Philippine home, preferred getting into a family where there were children, they wanted to make friends, to bring a few luxuries from camp, a little extra food or chocolate. Then, "Sure, there are the bucks, but I'll wager they're in the minority, far in the minority. No, I shall not declare Manila out of bounds to our soldiers, I won't." Then after a minute or two, "One more thing, you've got some pretty good medicine for those diseases now, haven't you?"

I lost that round and I reported General MacArthur's decision to General Dennit, the theater surgeon, and to Drs. Moore and Sternberg before they went back to Washington. The venereal disease rate continued to climb, but not much more. It had come close to its peak and, with the normal efforts on the parts of the doctors of the companies and the regiments, and the line officers conscious of the rate, it was gradually brought down to a more acceptable level. For me there was an important lesson, a lesson in perspective.

During this time the General liked to get away from his office, away from headquarters business which now focused on the upcoming Kyushu campaign. He would go out into the country in his jeep or car, usually alone with his driver. He might visit a division headquarters to discuss the mopping-up and to get a feel of his army. He also liked to travel through the familiar countryside, watching the Filipinos returning to their peacetime labors.

I went with him on two such occasions. He always asked the driver to go slowly when we passed through a barrio, that small poor village strung out for a couple of hundred yards along a secondary road. He would take in all of it and refer to details later in conversation.

As we were returning from my second trip with him, the General reminded me that we had not seen many poor barrios in the northern part of the Luzon plain. He said with feeling, "The people are poorer down here, very poor; they don't really own much of anything. Their livelihood depends on their work in the cane fields or the sugar *centrals*, both owned far away." He was silent for some time, then as we slowed for a barrio he pointed to some emaciated dogs, so much a part of the barrio scene. "Nobody owns any one of those dogs, Doc, but they are important to the village as a whole. They are its sewage system. But there are too many dogs—hounds for the available refuse. They call them barrio hounds; you don't see them much in the larger towns or cities."

He continued as he sometimes did in teaching me, "They all have worms and parasites. Notice how slow they are to rise at our approach, and how stiffly they get up. They walk as though it hurts, and they lie down again soon. They are starved, sick creatures."

One afternoon late, General MacArthur, returning from a sortie into the country, had a passenger with him. He handed me a small, thin, half-grown dirty dog and said, "Doc, this barrio hound caught me. He was lying half in a mud puddle as we came through one of those poor half-dead barrios. He cocked an ear at me and looked friendly, so I brought him home. He is a cunning little mutt. See if you can't get him cleaned up outside and probably inside and feed him up a bit. I want to keep him in the house."

We cleaned him up, dirt, fleas, lice, and mites on the outside, and worms and other parasites within. We let him eat his fill after a day or two, and he soon became a gay, affectionate puppy. The General named him Spotty, played with him, and the dog became his constant companion at home. He followed the General all through the house and greeted him with gusto when he returned in the evening. I was pleased with Spotty's attainment of a normal young-dog state and happy over his relationship with the General.

One day when the General was returning from the office for lunch, the guard came to smart attention as the car came up the driveway. While he stood there rigid, Spotty shot out of the house in front of him, eager to greet his friend, and was instantly killed under the left front wheel of the car as it came to a stop.

When the General realized what had happened and saw the guard still at stiff attention, he looked down at Spotty and then again at the guard as though he couldn't believe it. He let loose with a flow of invectives and profanity welling up from deep distress and from much younger days. The guard turned white and froze at attention, and the General suddenly broke off and went into the house.

Later, on the way back to the office, he said, "Guess I was a bit hard on that guard; perhaps you could let him know I am sorry and I dare say there was nothing he could have done; but I'm going to miss Spotty." I told him I had already gone to the guards' quarters and had reassured him; I mentioned also that the Corporal of the Guard told me the man was a new guard and had had it drilled into him what standing at attention means. This relieved the General, but he continued to miss Spotty; so in a week or so we made a foray into the country and got him another barrio hound, which he took to and named Blackie before we had even cleaned and fed him up. Blackie, spoiled by the General and the rest of the household, also became a very friendly dog; he gained our affection, and we all enjoyed his cavorting and warm greetings.

One morning a month or so later, the General said, "Doc, I sat up with Blackie last night. He's sick. Just as I was going to bed I heard him whine and I picked him up. He was shivering and he seemed to like to have me hold him, so I sat in that big chair with him most of the night. Why don't you take him to a veterinarian and find out what's wrong?" It was obvious that his rear legs were paralyzed, and paralysis probably meant distemper, but I took him to a veterinarian. We found a Filipino veterinary surgeon and later one of our own veterinary officers. They both diagnosed his sickness as distemper and said his hind legs would never work again. They also made the usual recommendation when a dog is paralyzed that way.

The General wondered if we couldn't do something about it. He held to the hope that Blackie might improve, so we rigged up, with the help of some of the guards, a pair of wheels for his rear end so that he could move about a bit by pulling himself with his front legs. Since he couldn't lie down until the wheels were removed, he took a bit of nursing. The guards gladly furnished this.

The General would say now and then, "You know, I heard Blackie last night. He sounded as if he were in pain." And I usually answered, "I am afraid he is, intermittently. The guard told me that he often whines at night." Two or three times I suggested that the best solution to Blackie's unhappiness would be to destroy him. The General always said, "Let's wait and see. He may get better."

The end of this story came later. When (in a few weeks) the Japanese requested a truce to discuss surrender, things moved very quickly—getting our headquarters ready to move to Tokyo, much calling to and from Washington, and the planning of post-surrender affairs.

The guard detail was moving with us, and though I made inquiries, I could find nobody else who wanted to take Blackie on. It was no time to give the General an additional problem, so I took it upon myself to put Blackie away. That wasn't easy for either of us. Once accomplished, I had to dispose of the body, which I did at night on a lonely road in a shallow grave behind a bamboo thicket.

A long time later—perhaps only two weeks, those first two weeks in Japan—I was in General MacArthur's office. He had asked me to go back to Manila with Dusty Rhoades to bring back Mrs. MacArthur and the others, and he had finished his few instructions to me. He sat quietly for a while, at his desk. Obviously he hadn't finished. Then he looked up again and said, "Now, Doc, about Blackie."

I quickly interrupted him. "Blackie is dead."

"What!"

"Yes sir, I killed him, I put him away. He was in more pain, comforting didn't relieve it, so I put him to sleep the night before we left Manila."

He looked at me with amazement. For a few seconds I thought I had made a grave mistake. Then his face relaxed and he said, "I guess you were right, Doc—thank you."

16

From Manila

On the 9th of June, aboard the *Boise* again, enroute to landings with the Australian troops at Brunei Bay, Borneo, we stopped at Puerta Princessa on the western Philippine island of Palawan. I didn't know his purpose until the General entered a long hut with an elevated floor along one side, with cubicles—iron barred cages much like the lion houses in the old-fashioned zoos. Standing at attention beside their cots on which lay their toilet articles open for inspection were ten or twelve very serious, aristocratic looking men, men high in the Philippines social, financial and political hierarchy.

"These were the men I used to see frequently, socially or on business. They were friends in a way," he said as we entered. "The Philippine government has accused them of collaboration with the Japanese."

Then he started down the line of cages. It was quiet and dramatic as he walked slowly through, stopping at each cell, looking at the man within, usually making a slight unsmiling nod and on one occasion looking impassively at the man behind the bars. To one he said, almost in an aside, "I saw your son the other day. He is well and sends his love to you."

He stopped briefly at the door. Nodding, he said, "That third man—we used to play chess fairly regularly. That fifth one was a Justice of the Supreme Court of the Philippines. He has an intriguing mind, and I much enjoyed wide-

171

ranging talk with him." He referred to others and of their high positions in the social and political structure of the Philippines. These civic leaders in the pre-war Philippines had been accused of profiting financially or of attaining power during the Japanese occupation.

After the visit he talked with the prison physician, inquiring after their health. Then outside we were alone together for a few minutes. He looked even more serious and said, "You know, there are people who think Roxas [General Manuel Roxas y Acuna] should be in there. He operated at a high level and he did deal with the Japanese. There are many others who think he should not. As you know, this has been of some concern to me."

He lowered his voice. "I have spoken with a number of people who were here through the occupation, and I have spoken with him several times. I have decided that the work he did with, or under, the Japanese was of a positive help to the Philippines and the Filipino people, and I urged the Philippine government not to look on him as a collaborator."

He tapped my chest with his forefinger and continued, "The Philippines need him as a leader and you mark, they will soon use him. The people love him, and I have confidence in him as a man." He had been talking intently and this had kept the rest of the party away. Now he relaxed; this episode was over. We joined the others and returned to the ship. He never mentioned Roxas to me again. General Roxas continued to be a hero of the Philippine people. At the end of the war he was elected President of the Philippine Commonwealth and became the first President of the new Republic in 1946.

Two weeks earlier General MacArthur had said on the way to the office, "Doc, the Australians are going to land in Borneo and I am going down to join them. I haven't been with them in any of their major actions. I want to watch and have them know of my interest." He had then reminisced. He warmly admired the fighting qualities, the courage and tenacity of the Australian Imperial Divisions.

Signal Corps, U.S. Army

The General with General Roxas (later President of the Philippines) and Presidente Osmeña.

"We'll be landing with the 9th, the division that fought that long Kokoda trail advance to the north coast of New Guinea from Moresby. Remember? They then had that grudging retreat, grudging all the way, when we couldn't meet them at Buna with our 32nd. That was shortly after I took over the Allied command."

My thoughts went back to the time when both I and the 32nd Division were freshly arrived in Australia. The division, which consisted of National Guardsmen from Michigan and Wisconsin, had to be readied for jungle fighting preparatory to shipping them off to occupy Buna, the last possible strategic site north of New Guinea's backbone of mountains. Their departure was delayed by the behavior of the Australian longshoremen loading the ships. These men could not be hurried; they stopped work for a cloud in the distance, their "cuppa" for tea break, for any excuse to slow down. I was told at the time that this dilly-dallying detained our ships and men in port for seven or eight days. General MacArthur was urged to use our troops to load the ships, but he refused because he felt it would be an invasion of Australian sovereignty. As it turned out, the Japanese landed at Buna just three days before our troops, en route at last in their belated ships, were due to arrive at that objective. They had to turn back. This failure later cost us three or four months of hard fighting to take the site.

This early respect for the Australians was undoubtedly important in gaining the country's warm-hearted cooperation in the Pacific war, after they had been bled out in the North African desert. I believe Australia was our only ally whose lend-lease balance was in our favor.

The next morning we stood off Brunei Bay, Borneo, and after a long and heavy bombardment went ashore with the Australian troops of the 1st Corps under the command of General Mooreshead. The shelling had been aimed well inland, and so the beach area had a peacetime look, including two wooden signs. One, weathered but not as old as its message, said: "On this spot are buried seven seamen from

H.M.S. Bounty." The other one pointed, and read, "To the Golf Course."

The General found out where the resistance was, and off we went until we met it. General Kenney profanely, and a more polite General Mooreshead, finally persuaded the General to turn back; several hours later, after talking with General Mooreshead and his staff, we were again aboard ship.

On the way back to Manila we stopped off at the island of Jolo in the Sulu Archipelago to make it possible for the Sultan of Sulu to call on General MacArthur. Here was a bare hill where Black Jack Pershing had made his name, charging up it, during the Moro insurrection. Since that time the militant Moros had been peaceful friends because of financial support given to the Sultan, their spiritual and temporal leader, by the United States and Great Britain.

We wanted to show him respect; so after touring the hilly island with the U.S. colonel commanding our forces there, we stopped in a pleasant palm grove near the little dock, General MacArthur, General Eichelberger, the colonel, and I. While waiting for the Sultan to arrive, the colonel lent the General his field glasses, of which he seemed very proud, to scan the hill Pershing had taken, and to look at an area along the shore where his troops had met some resistance.

The Sultan came, wearing the light gray pants common in India that resemble our winter underwear. His shirt, of similar material, was simply embroidered and a dark sash worn bandolier fashion completed his dress. His head was bare with close cropped hair, accentuating the smallness of his body and even the wrinkles on his face. With him was his vizier—or chancellor of the exchequer—similarly dressed, and possibly a few years younger. But firmly clutched in the Sultan's left hand was the right hand of a little boy, five or six years old, his grandson, obviously favored and cherished. The Sultan almost seemed to consult him at times.

General MacArthur received the Sultan with warmth and respect, and they exchanged a few words in English. Then the vizier helped carry along a conversation with much emphasis on nouns and adjectives. Finally, with solemnity, the Sultan presented the General with a beautiful filigreed silver-handled knife, a ceremonial Moro bolo.

As he accepted and admired it, the General gave General Eichelberger a quick glance. He in turn took an anxious look around, but not for long. He relaxed as his eyes settled on those beautiful field glasses hanging from the colonel's neck. He reached over as though to borrow them. The colonel gladly handed them over; General Eichelberger gave them ceremoniously to General MacArthur, who presented them with dignity and elan to the Sultan, who was indeed happy and immediately tried them out. The pleased look on the colonel's face changed to surprise and then to a youthful chagrin as he realized he had really been had.

We soon went down to the dock and I, being junior, jumped into the small boat first. The others didn't follow, but continued to talk in a close little group: the Sultan, his vizier, and the two generals. My eyes were now at ankle level and I was fascinated by the touch of pantomime that ensued. The little boy let go his grandfather's hand, opened his pants, and pissed generously over the legs and feet of the four who were almost surrounding him. They continued their desultory conversation as though discussing matters of state. Possibly they were.

I later asked the General if he was aware of what was happening. "Yes, I felt and heard it, but the Sultan was more exposed than I, and he kept looking at me as the vizier translated; and that little pisser *was* the apple of his eye."

Several weeks later we joined the Aussies again in Borneo, landing with them at Balikapapen, the large oil refinery in the southeast part of the island. Again the bombardment lasted a long time as though we were telling the Aussies, "We're here." It was dramatic. The oil tanks made tantalizing targets and were blown up with satisfying explosions. Rivers of oil came down the hill, some of them burning, and black smoke rose many miles into the sky.

Waiting for the end of the bombardment and for the first wave to go ashore, the General went into his cabin and soon wondered mildly if I could get a chocolate ice cream soda or sundae from the canteen. I went far below deck where all seemed deserted and finally found the ice-cream counter and then a sailor who, when he heard whom the sundae was for, quickly opened up and produced two beauties. I took them up to the General. We were just putting our spoons in for the first bite when an eager-beaver, excited idiot came rushing in and shouted, "You can't go ashore now, General. The enemy is putting a heavy barrage on the beach." That ended our sundaes; General MacArthur put his down, I got one bite of mine, and we were in a landing craft headed for shore in less than two minutes.

The sand and the water were popping up all over the place towards which we were heading. The barrage stopped just before we reached it and we soon touched bottom on a sand bar. I jumped off into what I hoped was shallow water and disappeared. It was a deep spot. I got ashore; the barge moved sideways a hundred feet or so and came well in to land. We climbed the hill between rivulets of oil, some burning. On top, after passing a company of Australian soldiers, we reached an open ridge. It was good for viewing and for being viewed. The Aussies kept saying, "E'll do me," and other more earthy but good things about General MacArthur. A number asked me if I had come unstuck.

As we stood on that open ridge looking inland at the burning and destruction, a sniper started placing bullets pretty close to us, ten or twenty feet away. The General continued to stand, looking searchingly inland with his hands in his hip pockets. The rest of the party kept looking a bit worriedly at him. I felt worse about this modest danger than I had about most of my other forward experiences. I thought it might be my last landing before going home, and a particularly bad time to be hit. One of the American colonels with us must have felt the same way—he decided to sit down. I looked at him sitting and at the General standing,

On the island of Jolo the Sultan of Sulu calls on General MacArthur with the governor of Jolo and his camera-shy grandson.

Lord Louis Mountbatten and the General.

worked up a bit of anger, and sat down. The General then decided to come down the hill.

Soon back aboard the *Cleveland* the General said, "Doc, how would you like a chocolate sundae?" I went down and got two apiece, which we finished.

After dinner when I was taking a ribbing from the others for my ducking, the General broke in, "That's all right. Doc was trying to help me, and I appreciate it."

The following afternoon we were back in Manila.

17

Jean and the General

"It's been seven weeks and five days since I said goodbye to Jean, Doc . . . I miss her," and then the General and I talked a bit about her and about Arthur. This conversation was on his little porch in Tacloban, but he would mention the days every few weeks when the two of us were sitting alone after dinner, usually on a porch or a veranda. It was a long stretch from the middle of October, when we finally left Brisbane for good, until March, when the freighter brought Jean and Arthur and the others up to Manila. General MacArthur particularly resented the necessity of separation at his age. He was not unaware of the years I had been away from my wife, Meg, and our children, but he explained it once: "Doc, you have a long life ahead of you, time to enjoy and appreciate each other. I can't count too many years."

Her many, many friends love Jean MacArthur, but they probably know little of her life during the war; of her living in a house on top of the "Rock" (Corregidor) until a few days before the Japanese finally destroyed it with artillery and bombs. They probably don't know of her life in the Malinta Tunnel, (that garrison within the rock of Corregidor) under siege, or the details of the escape in the P.T. boat commanded by Lieutenant John Bulkley through the Japanese fleet on that moonless night after leaving the little dock at the foot of Corregidor. She never talks of the flight in a bomber through enemy-controlled skies from the island of Minda-

184

nao, the great southern island of the Philippines, to Australia. I am sure she rarely mentions her life in Brisbane, when she couldn't very well have many friends. There she regularly went out shopping for food for the General and Arthur, and often prepared it. In grocery store lines, she was usually recognized and always urged to go to the front of the line, but she never did, preferring to wait and chat with the other housewives. She was—is—a charming hostess, positive, good-natured, outgoing. Her laugh is warm.

One of many glimpses into her life comes to mind. In Brisbane, where the MacArthurs lived on the top floor of Lennons Hotel, a guard was stationed at the door to their apartment, for protocol or security. I was certainly aware of his standing smartly at attention whenever I went to the apartment. I had also noticed a chair and a small table with magazines within a few feet of the door. They seemed incongruous until I learned once from the captain in charge of guard details that Mrs. MacArthur had put them there and also that she often brought out a cup of chocolate (not coffee) for the guard on duty in the late evening. On a recent visit with Mrs. MacArthur when a color guard marching through the hotel lobby reminded me of the Lennons' guard, I asked her how the General had reacted to her consideration for the guards. She was delighted with the question, for one of those guards had just called on her and she had a story to tell; two stories, really.

"Doc, I thought of those guards standing out there all night and I knew there were probably regulations and rules about it—and all—and I didn't want to fight regulations, so I said to the General, 'I don't want to know too much about military rules or etiquette, but I do consider the hall outside our apartment as my domain.' Then I put the chair and table out. He never referred to it!"

She loves to tell anecdotes about the General, so she went into the next part: "Just a few weeks ago those soldiers—those guards—held a reunion and they wrote me some very nice letters. One of them came to call on me just last week.

He wanted particularly to tell me a story. He said that one of the guards, late in the evening, sat down for a minute in the chair outside our door. The next thing he knew, he felt something brush lightly across his knees; he came to with a jerk and saw the General opening the door and entering the apartment. He didn't turn around, but it was his hand that had brushed across the guard's knees. The guard was so worried that he reported it to the officer of the guard, who took a long look at him and finally said, 'You're a lucky son of a gun! If that had been a second louie instead of that particular four-star general who had found you asleep at your post, you would have been court-martialed.' "

Jean Faircloth MacArthur was deeply important to the General. She was a confidante with whom he could discuss, or in front of whom he could talk about, the people with whom he worked, the General Headquarters staff, and those coming out from Washington. He needed to talk about his officers and his visitors and he needed somebody with whom he could talk of the overall strategy—his strategy, in dealing with Washington, vis-à-vis the Navy, and even vis-à-vis the Japanese. In different senses these were all a part of the strategy of war viewed at his level. Up to a point, he could do this with General Sutherland, his Chief of Staff, but as the war went on and Captain Z intruded more and more, he did this less and less. With Jean as a listener he talked of plans, of people, of anything that came to mind. To a different degree he did this with me in the jeep or of an evening when we were in the field. He once said, "Good talk, it was a bit like talking with Jean," and I felt I had received a heartfelt compliment.

Visitors would try to lead Mrs. MacArthur into conversations about the war, wanting a peek into what might be coming up. She had a uniform answer. With an engaging smile she would say, "Well, all I know is what I read in the newspapers," and then she would quote from a recent news article, never enlarging. After one visit from a Washington dignitary who was rude in pressing her to talk about the war in our area, she said to me with a conspiratorial look, "Old so-and-so was certainly trying to worm something out of me, wasn't he?"

General MacArthur wouldn't visit a hospital in spite of my frequent invitations and urgings. He finally explained: he felt a responsibility for those sick and wounded men, his men, so intense that a handshake or a pat on the shoulder seemed a shallow and paltry gesture. He couldn't afford the emotional toll. "But why don't you take Jean to visit the hospitals? The men would rather see her anyhow." So I asked her and found that she wanted very much to visit the hospitals and talk with the men there. In spite of her modesty, I am sure she sensed how much the soldiers liked and appreciated her presence.

We began visiting a few general hospitals in Manila. I would arrange a time a few days ahead, and when we arrived the commanding officer already knew that she preferred to visit with the men by herself or with the doctor caring for them. She always wore white gloves, I presumed in true Southern tradition. We would accompany her to the ward, and after introductions the ward doctor usually took her around from bed to bed. Occasionally I would go along for a while, but usually I stayed behind and talked with the C.O.

As she went from bed to bed, from wounded soldier to wounded soldier, she would shake the patient's hand, saying, "I am Jean MacArthur. I am sorry you are in the hospital. I hope they are taking good care of you." Or, "What part of the country are you from?" With some more comfortable talkers she stayed longer than with others. She would talk with a hundred patients or more on one of these visits.

Afterwards she liked to talk in general terms about the hospital. She sensed its atmosphere with keen perception. And in a more spirited manner she would tell of particular soldiers. Once she referred to a soldier who had lost his leg below the knee and whose stump was up in traction. She said, "He wouldn't look at me, turned his head away. Do you think he was angry or resentful, or maybe he was embarrassed? He was young enough to be embarrassed. I felt so sorry for him," and after a pause, "but he's through with the war now." She was definitely interested in the soldiers as individuals and, as far as she could, shared their problems.

After visiting two or three general hospitals, she said, "Doc, can't we go forward? Visit these men earlier after they've been wounded?" I agreed to that; so we went a bit forward and visited a station hospital. These are smaller hospitals farther forward in the hospital chain than the general hospitals. They are more limited in what they can do, primarily by the relatively short time they are allowed to hold a patient and by lack of a number of specialty services.

We then went to a smaller hospital, a field hospital supporting the action in a sector east of Manila. She wanted to visit ever more forward. I thought she wanted to share danger. I finally took her to a small field hospital supporting a regiment in action northeast of Manila. It had been under enemy shell-fire the night before. When we arrived, we were met by the C.O. and part of the regimental band at the flagpole. The band greeted us with a few goose-flesh-prompting martial pieces. The obvious delight and enthusiasm among the men and patients was heartwarming, and Mrs. MacArthur's broad smile camouflaged tears. I heard words and phrases: "His wife"—"Coming here"—"Beautiful"—"Our hospital"—"Just look at her!" Here in tents and temporary huts—flag flying at the flagstaff out front, a few flowers in a bed that antedated the hospital—here were recently wounded soldiers and some who were convalescing. The band continued to play with gusto until we went in. While she was visiting, more wounded were brought in. She was aware of that activity. As she went from bed to bed, there was an informal feeling; this was their hospital, those soldiers', that regiment's, different from a larger hospital, and they welcomed her. The patients were eager to talk with her, and her face reflected their feelings of pleasure, seriousness, sadness over a loss, a buddy, or a limb.

As we left, she became wistful; before we drove off she

Jean MacArthur and her husband, the General, below the bow of the *Bataan*.

looked long at the foothills a few miles away where the fighting was going on. I think she wanted to go that way. As we drove off, her eyes were wide and glistening, and her expression was one of partial fulfillment. She had been close to soldiers, within an hour of their being "hit." She envied those who could care for them. In a sense, these were her "men." And she knew she had helped them, raised the morale. She was excited.

The next morning the General called me in, looked at me hard and very seriously. He was angry. "I take it from Jean that you went pretty far forward with her yesterday. You took her to a hospital under intermittent enemy fire. I don't like it!" He hit the desk with his fist and his eyes flashed. "You can't, you mustn't expose her like that. You know what Jean means to me and how I need her. If anything should happen to her while you were taking her forward,"—he searched for strong words—"I don't know just what I would do to you!" He pounded the desk once more. "Don't ever do that again!"

This criticism was personal, not military, and the way he looked at me I felt sure that what he would have done would have been done personally—not through any court-martial procedure. It was a short, threatening dressing down and the only one he ever gave me.

General MacArthur needed Jean for the simple, profound sustaining qualities of her love for him, her faith in him, her quiet satisfaction in listening to him when he needed to talk without constraint or explanation to a trusted and intimate companion. Her pride in him has always been deep, real, and often expressed. From her he drew strength.

18

The End of the Fighting

On August 7th when we arrived at the entrance to GHQ, we were given a copy of *Stars and Stripes*, an extra edition stating across its front page: "Atom Bomb Dropped," as though we should know what an atomic bomb was. It was explained, along with a description of the probable damage it had caused to the Japanese industrial city of Hiroshima.

General MacArthur stopped and read, then slowly and silently climbed the stairs, took another look at the paper, then murmured, "That's far beyond anything you can imagine. They will think it's supernatural." He didn't say directly whether he had known of it in advance, or known something about it, but I rather think he did. He thought and he talked about the bomb in his office. Impressed, awed by the vast destruction from one bomb, he said, as we were driving home that first day after Hiroshima, "This will end the war. It will seem superhuman—almost supernatural—and will give the Emperor and the Japanese people a face-saving opportunity to surrender. You watch, they'll ask for it pretty quick." And they did.

As he always did, he looked much farther ahead, to future wars. "With such weapons, a large standing army is not going to be of much use. A war would be over before it could be brought into action. What we shall need is a small, highly mobile, highly technically-trained army."

As he had done earlier, he spoke again of a peacetime draft. "The training of a large number of civilians in the rudiments of military science is very expensive and gives a false sense of accomplishment and is something that wouldn't be very useful." He said that such broadly scattered money should be used instead in creating a small, highly-skilled professional army: "The infantry won't be slogging up to any front—there probably will be no front. The weapons will be increasingly complicated. It will take intelligent men to plan their use and highly-trained, intelligent men to use them. We need to have such an army. Pay it well, well enough to take people from industry, from General Motors, from U.S. Steel. We must get it where it is needed, overnight, and we must keep it technically superior."

When he later saw the planned suicidal defenses about Tokyo Bay, hole to hole, tunnel on tunnel, networks of tunnels, he said, "Those bombs that ended the war saved us about 500,000 casualties. I think the Japanese would have sacrificed at least a million."

He spoke of the atomic bomb always with great solemnity, never dropped his air of awe and portent. He once said, "For a large war we must learn warfare over again, strategy, tactics, speed in communication, in transportation. We need imagination!"

Later, in Japan, one day on the way to the office, he was reminiscing about the Philippine campaign. "It was hard on the civilian population; but if we have warfare using the atomic bomb, the cities will disappear, and that's where the civilians are."

In August we heard rumors that the Japanese were seeking a truce, that a Japanese plane would shortly arrive in Manila. I called General Willoughby's office for confirmation, and finally got someone who recognized my voice and told me, "Yes, in two hours at Nichols Field." I got hold of Dave Chambers and Dusty Rhoades and we went to the field to join three or four hundred others who had wind of the occasion. A Colonel Sidney F. Mashbir, who had lived in Japan and spoke Japanese, was there as the official greeter.

There we stood on a sunny afternoon on this small airfield in Manila, the remains of recent destruction still evident. We stood and we looked and we listened. Unless one is trained or is told where to look, a plane can be very close before one spots it. The younger men saw it first and pointed, not with happy excitement. They were serious and intent. The plane came in and quickly landed. It was one of our DC-4's to which the Japanese emissaries had transferred at Ei Jima.

When it came to a stop about fifty yards away, the door was quickly opened. I still couldn't believe that Japanese would come out, but they did, and Colonel Mashbir went to the plane to greet them. There they were, six, eight, twelve and more Japanese men in uniform coming down the steps onto the concrete. As the engines stopped, Mashbir stepped forward, reached out his hand for a handshake with the first man, and then, as he told me later, he decided he shouldn't be shaking hands and changed the motion into a gesture indicating where they should go, leaving the Japanese official's hand dangling.

We watched as these small, grave men were escorted by Colonel Mashbir and a few other officers and M.P.'s to four or five waiting cars which quickly took off for some rendezvous, probably not at GHQ.

We looked at each other. This must be what we had been waiting for for three and a half years! Could it be true? Should we jump? We didn't. We returned to our usual duties.

The General didn't say much on his way home that evening. I am sure he was lost in the plans for the post-surrender era in Japan. Perhaps he was looking back, for as we got out of the car, he said, "No more shooting, Doc, no more shooting." Then after a pause, "Good night."

The next morning General MacArthur suggested I accompany him to a briefing by his staff, describing the terms of the truce. About twenty of his officers were assembled in a room that couldn't have held many more. The requests and proposals of both sides were discussed. In a sense, these were housekeeping details, for the Japanese were surrendering. We were told of a schedule of demobilization and of sequential zones of demilitarization. All was logical and orderly until it came to a puzzling Japanese request to keep a large number of rifles, machine guns, and cannon, along with appropriate ammunition, at or near the Atsugi airdrome, some miles south of Tokyo. Why?

The explanation lay in the training of the dedicated Japanese kamikaze pilots. Having sworn to die in destroying their enemy for the Emperor and their country, fifty thousand of these men were now encamped near Atsugi. The Japanese command was not sure how quickly the Emperor could persuade them that the war was over and that they must renounce their determination to sacrifice themselves. They might need this equipment to keep them in line. After discussion, we agreed to the request.

The first steps towards peace between our countries had been taken. It had been taken with serious calm. We were too close to wartime memories to feel exultant. What would the second step be—and when?

19

Japan

On August 29th Dusty Rhoades brought General MacArthur up to Okinawa. I joined him there, having come up the previous day with Ben Whipple and a load of documents.

The General established himself in temporary quarters and in the late afternoon received a number of visitors. They were military visitors, but social visits, respects, and greetings from generals who had come up in other planes and who would be continuing to Japan the next day.

In the early evening, Jack Sverdrup came in, just back from the States. He told me that "yesterday" President Truman had asked him to become Secretary of the Army. He was going in to tell the General, who he knew would want him to accept. Jack didn't want that position at this time. With the war over he wanted to stay until General MacArthur released him, and then he wanted to return as quickly as possible to his civilian work, engineering and construction. He took a deep breath as he went in to talk with the General. When he came out about an hour later, looking subdued, he let out another deep breath. He said the General had urged him almost vehemently to accept the appointment, for he felt he would then have at least one friend "in court." During the war I am sure Jack would have accepted a "suicidal" assignment, had General MacArthur asked him, but now with the war over, the priorities were already changing, as they were for me and others not of the Regular Army.

By the end of this very full day we were all anxious to get on. We were impatient to see the homeland of the men we had been fighting these many years. We had begun to grasp, through talk, new and changed plans, and the interval of time since the truce, that the war was really over and we were on our way to feel that reality by entering their country and by witnessing some official signing. We felt happier now; somehow we could allow ourselves that. The General, however, continued more aloof, apart from our prevailing mood. One could tell he was stewing. He would pace, hands in his hip pockets, get his long-stemmed corncob pipe filled, light it, and hold it in his right hand, letting it go out. He would sit down and then he would change his position, cross his legs and a little later uncross them. There was no doubt his thoughts were far away from us and his mind active.

The following morning there was a great sense of expectancy as he again boarded the *Bataan*. This was a brand new *Bataan*, a C-54 which Dusty had been putting through its paces for several weeks. Up from the field and out over the ocean, we headed north. The direction itself was exciting. General MacArthur soon relaxed into his window seat, on the port side of the plane, riding backwards. It seemed only a short time until we were sighting land again, to our left, then ahead, and we passed over the beaches of southern Honshu. The General had been alternately animated and thoughtful. He looked almost eagerly out of the window as we came up over that southern shore of this, the main island. This was apparently a resort area; the General figured out and named a few of the places below us. Then, as we continued north over the island, he decided he had seen enough. He knew he would have a busy afternoon, and took a nap. He was napping when we came upon Fujiyama, the symbol of Japan to so many. About then, Dusty came back and took him up to the cockpit. On this beautifully clear day, there, a few miles off our port side, was the startling, exciting, snow-capped cone. That, more than the landing itself, told me we had arrived.

We landed at Atsugi Air Base at 2 P.M. Neither large nor impressive, it lay about sixty miles south of Tokyo near the edge of the first demilitarized zone. Six hundred of our airborne troops had landed here during the morning, along with a few other planes carrying the vanguard of the dignitaries who would participate in the surrender ceremonies. I don't believe our Navy had yet entered Tokyo Bay. There had been heated discussions, the Navy wanting no Japanese fishing boats in the bay for obvious reasons, and the General stating that the people needed their food almost desperately, and that he had the Emperor's word nothing would happen. He won. The Japanese fished, and the Navy entered the bay.

By the end of the day there were 6,000 American troops in the area; within two or three miles of us there were 50,000 kamikazes behind barbed wire, and within thirty or forty miles of us at least two million Japanese troops, under arms. Some months later, Sir Winston Churchill characterized this as MacArthur's most dangerous landing—and at the time of the landing there were many who were deeply concerned about the risks. However, General MacArthur knew he had the Emperor's word and he trusted it, trusted it as the Emperor's honor and trusted the strength of the Emperor's word to control the Japanese people, including their army. Our Administration worried him more than the power of the Emperor's word. "I just hope the President and the Pentagon realize to some small degree how important the Emperor of Japan is to the Japanese transition; transition not only from war to peace, but from feudal state to democracy." This he had said several times, and had elaborated on it to me when he discussed his plans for the future of Japan. It continued to worry him, and he spoke of it almost to himself.

Enthusiasm now came in waves. Our warm and happy greetings and hand pumpings with those who had arrived shortly before us overwhelmed the ritual courtesies of the Japanese officially there to welcome us.

We were soon put into taxis and private cars (no military transportation), fifteen or twenty vehicles. We made a small

Signal Corps, U.S. Army

The General takes the first step on to Japanese soil at Atsugi airport
after the end of the war. August 30, 1945.

The General and his staff, shortly after their arrival at Atsugi Airport, Japan, August 30, 1945. Left to right General Aikin, Colonel Rhoades, General Sutherland, General Byers, General MacArthur, and General Eichelberger.

convoy heading for the Grand Hotel in Yokohama about thirty miles away. As we drove through this flat countryside, there were Japanese soldiers stationed every fifty yards or so along the road. They were on both sides of the road, twenty or thirty feet off it, backs to the road, rifles at the ready, looking out over the fields. Was their facing away a token of respect or an oriental indication of defeat, or was it necessary precaution? I assumed it was the latter, and thought it a good idea.

We passed villages on the way, but saw no people and the countryside looked peaceful. From our cars we gained no feeling of a country at war. Then as we neared Yokohama we came through a small town, a suburb perhaps, with only one or two buildings standing. The rest were all rubble. Flat, it appeared blown up and burned down. Small "house" or "block" factories here and there were indicated by ruined machinery standing in the wreckage. We had done this; it must have been a successful raid. Where were the people now? Where had they been when it happened? Was I feeling concern for our enemy of a few days ago?

As we entered the outskirts of Yokohama we saw terrible destruction. It was a chaotic mess, yet orderly in the sense that one could make out the blocks, bounded by streets or roads. The buildings hadn't been high enough to fall across them. These outlines emphasized the massive total devastation that lay about us. Here and there a standing building of concrete showed by its starkness and contrast the extent of the rubble that lay about it. In the city were small areas of several blocks here and there that had escaped damage. The Grand Hotel was in one such area. A mile or so in from the waterfront a low ridge covered with European type houses also seemed to have escaped. Eighty percent of Yokohama had been destroyed by explosives and fire bombs.

The Grand Hotel was near the harbor, a square European style hotel of the nineteen twenties, with a dark lobby in the twenties style. General MacArthur was given a suite at the front of the hotel on the third or fourth floor. I drew a room near him, and Larry and I joined him for a late lunch in his quarters.

What does one talk about at the first meal in a country which has just surrendered after three and a half years of heavy fighting? What does the Commander-in-Chief of the victorious armies talk about? Not of the forthcoming surrender ceremony; that was still in the writing and rewriting phase. Not of the work ahead in the transition for Japan; that was still his private arena where he could set plans up and knock them down and rearrange them, and only in exasperation or satisfaction give us a peep in now and then. No, the talk was of the things at hand. The General was eager to know what Tokyo looked like; what it had to offer in buildings, facilities that we could use. He was awed by the very great destruction in Yokohama; awed and, I thought, disturbed. I brought up my first impression from the trip in. He said, "Doc, those were successful raids, and the recon planes showed that—at great distance. We needed those raids, but when you see the results from the street level as we did just now, it brings in to you the horror of war, total war. Those were civilians working and living there."

As we ate soup, bread and butter, and some cold meat, he said, "Charles (General Willoughby) tells me the Japanese are close to hunger. They sorely need meat or fish or soybeans. The effects of war must have accelerated terrifically for them in the past four or five months."

As we finished eating, he asked me to get Colonel Mashbir and go into Tokyo to see what the status of the American Embassy was, to take a look at the Imperial Hotel, pay a courtesy call at the Swiss Embassy, and see what possibilities there were for an office building for GHQ. He knew that Tokyo was out of bounds to American troops, but suggested we get an official from the Japanese Foreign Office to accompany us, to show us the way, and presumably to give an appearance of acceptance.

When they heard about it, Jack Sverdrup and Pat Casey joined us and as engineers had good reason to. I was of course delighted to have them. Jack and I rode in one taxi with a Foreign Office man, and Mashbir and Pat in a second taxi. We started off just after lunch. The twenty-five miles from the Grand Hotel in Yokohama to the center of Tokyo was a vast area of destruction. Between seventy and eighty percent of the buildings had been destroyed, burned, bombed; there was much evidence of small machine shops again, and of neighborhood factories among the ruins; there were big tank-like affairs here and there which the Foreign Service Officer said were filled with water and were for the Japanese to jump into in case of fire bombing. Yokohama burned, and he just said flatly, the tanks didn't work.

This was our first chance to talk with a Japanese official, so we asked him a number of questions. "Would they have continued to fight if it hadn't been for the atomic bomb?" "Ah, yes." "How were they holding out with food?" "No trouble." (We had heard otherwise.) After a few more Jack said, "What did you think of Pearl Harbor?" His quick answer was, "It was a very successful attack, but we made a grave mistake in not going right on to the coast of California." That stopped us for while.

Nearing the center of Toyko, we were soon virtually surrounded by Japanese troops. We were probably not far from a station of the railway our road was paralleling. According to the armistice agreement, Tokyo was still in Japanese hands until their troops—about two million—could be evacuated, a matter of a week or ten days. These troops around us were on their way to the trains that would take them away from the city for demobilization, but meanwhile we Americans in our two taxis were there on their sufferance. Our driver, apparently antagonistic towards them or us, honked his horn and speeded up as we approached twenty or thirty streaming across the road. This aggressiveness prompted Japanese officers on two occasions to reach for their revolvers, whereupon we reached for ours. Had we been Japanese, I dare say those officers would have shot us, but nothing happened.

We were still easing out of our tenseness when we found

the American Embassy. The office part of it (the chancellery) had received a hit with minor damage; the living quarters were in good condition. Next, we paid the Swiss Embassy a courtesy call. It was an intriguing experience; the Swiss were absolutely noncommittal in look and word. We learned from their air of faultless neutrality that there had been a war and it looked as though Japan had lost. We then went to look at office buildings. The Dai Ichi, a large insurance building across from the Imperial Palace grounds, was unhurt and could hold our GHQ and the headquarters of the Supreme Commander for the Allied Powers (S.C.A.P.)

We then visited the famous Imperial Hotel, the Frank Lloyd Wright building that had survived the great Tokyo earthquake. It had survived the war, too, except for a small corner at the back that was gone. We entered the lobby to make inquiry. A group of five Japanese who were having tea in a corner evaporated when they saw us. We felt just a bit like bullies.

In the evening we returned to Yokohama. We had thought that this would be a comfortable ride in the dark, but when we got in the taxi the driver turned on a bright light in the top shining right down on us. We could not get him to turn it off, for apparently ever since a bomb had been thrown at the Japanese Emperor from the back seat of a taxicab all cars had to have the back seat well lighted after dark. "It was the law," so said our Foreign-Office man. And so we drove through the streets of Tokyo with thousands upon thousands of soldiers and civilians milling around, and certainly looking at us. For the soldiers I doubt there was much sadness, even in defeat. Street lights showed that many were happy, hand in hand with their girls.

Had the roles been reversed, say in Australia or the U.S., and with thousands carrying guns, there would surely have been several who couldn't resist the temptation of shooting the recent enemy.

The next morning the General agreed that our evening experience was good evidence of the great authority of the Emperor. After hearing our report, General MacArthur decided to move into the Embassy as soon as Tokyo was cleared of troops. We could use the Imperial Hotel and another for the officers quarters and establish the non-commissioned officers and men in other hotels and buildings and in camps set up in nearby parks. He also made the decision to use the Dai Ichi building to house our combined headquarters.

That evening, the second evening at the Grand Hotel, moved from polite conversation to an emotional climax. Some of our allies joined us for dinner in a private dining room in the basement of the hotel. There were no windows, and a low ceiling. Twenty or twenty-five of us sat at a long table. The food was all prepared by the Japanese staff and was good: fish, rice, steak, vegetables and soup. The steak surprised me. We had not brought it with us.

There was a feeling of exhilaration among the Americans. We were all allies and had fought long and lost many lives in this struggle, but this final carry through to Tokyo had been primarily our push. Our Army, Navy and Air Force had furnished over ninety percent of this muscle.

Now in addition to the expanded Bataan group, there were also Australians, Canadians, British and Soviet officers, and we were struggling with banal talk with our allies.

My back towards the door, I was seated across the table from four or five of our veterans of Bataan. Soon after we sat down, those across the table looked to the door almost in unison. A look of disbelief, then surprise and joy, came over their faces, and they all jumped up to welcome a very thin but well-looking older officer: Lieutenent General Jonathan M. "Skinny' Wainwright, the man left behind to command Corregidor and Bataan when MacArthur had been ordered out by President Roosevelt; the man to whom MacArthur is quoted as saying, "Hang on and we'll be back to relieve you." He had finally surrendered his starved sick army and is said to have felt guilty for not carrying on. That had been over three years ago. Many of those prisoners held in camps or in Bilibid Prison in the Philippines had died of scurvy, dysentery, and starvation; but General Wainwright had been among the numbers sent to Manchuria, where, thanks probably to the soybeans, they were reasonably well-nourished. This must have accounted for his state of health.

There were no dry eyes among the Americans, just laughter, tears and I am sure a few words other than "Skinny!" General MacArthur was on his feet and welcomed and embraced General Wainwright. His eyes were moist as he embraced him, then held him off to look at, a hand on each shoulder, and then embraced him again.

The other nationals soon understood the meaning of the greetings and smiled appreciatively or in some sense applauded.

The meal and the evening continued on a different level and tone. A few cigars appeared after dinner and some liqueurs, and the questions and answers in both directions increased. MacArthur and the officers of our Allies left about ten o'clock, but the atmosphere of the old friends united again continued until late.

The General now wanted to get out of the Grand Hotel. He wanted a place where he could pace, move about and think, so in another day or two we moved to a house belonging to a large oil company, one of those on the ridge that had escaped harm. Here he could walk among several rooms and the living room was large and gracious, a good place to relax after dinner. Temporary offices were soon found for him in a building near the waterfront beyond the customs pier. Here he settled in for a few days before the move to Tokyo.

General MacArthur wrote and rewrote the words he would read at the surrender ceremony aboard the battleship *Missouri*. He was determined that it should be strong, not vindictive, but he was already looking beyond it. It was to become a step on the way to the rebuilding of Japan. He looked forward to his forthcoming conversations with the Emperor and referred to them several times. He was eager to get at the next big phase of his work in the Orient. He was anxious to move into the Embassy in Tokyo where he could receive the Emperor and open their discourse.

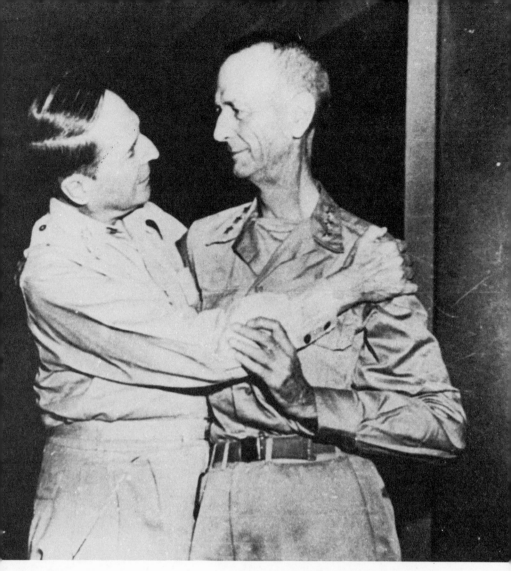

MacArthur greets General Wainwright in the basement dining room of the Grand Hotel in Yokohama on the evening before the surrender ceremony which took place September 2, 1945.

General MacArthur with General Percival, highest ranking British prisoner of war, and General Wainwright.

20

September 2, 1945

Driving down to the dock with General MacArthur on a spottily sunny morning for the surrender ceremony, I experienced a host of thoughts and feelings. One was awe. Also a deep relief as I realized that now many millions of people would no longer have to fight or risk injury and death, and could return home. Finally, I was grateful that I was alive and unwounded. These thoughts I had to arrange and push through my mind. At a lower level tears fought with anticipation of historic drama—the final act of a long play in which I was both actor and spectator.

We had gotten up before five, had a moderate American breakfast of eggs, bacon, toast, jam, and coffee in the dining room, where we found General Richardson (Commanding General of the Pacific Area), who had just flown in from his headquarters in Hawaii, sitting in a corner, alone and uncheered. I tried to make him feel warmly welcome, but we were soon embroiled in a number of last-minute decisions, details, and searches for people. At 7:20 we started off in the General's car, taking along Admiral John J. Ballentine.

The General didn't invite conversation on the five-minute ride through the cleared streets of Yokohama, through rubble-covered areas and the ruins of burnt-out houses and small factories, as we drove to the Customs House Pier. I am sure he too was dwelling on the significance of the occasion, with many recollections of how he had brought us to this point; but he was also thinking of the next step, the upcoming problems of dealing with the great nation we had defeated. Otherwise, why did he ask, out of the blue, if I knew whether General Sutherland was meeting a representative of the Emperor that afternoon?

We were met by an honor guard and a band; then we boarded the *Buchanan,* a destroyer, one of several vessels transporting the Americans and their Allies to the *Missouri* lying out in Tokyo Bay—General MacArthur, General Wainwright (looking happy in a subdued way, perhaps relieved after the welcome given him), General Doolittle, and Generals Whitehead and White of the 5th Air Force, and others. On the way out through the fleet, we enjoyed a second breakfast. Many small formations of our planes flew overhead and, together with the many fighting ships in the harbor, built up an impression of power and strength. On the way I had a chance to talk with Major John R. Pugh, who had been General Wainwright's aide throughout their three years of imprisonment. A very pleasant fellow, he didn't sound too badly harassed, and was amazingly relaxed. He thought the prisoners in Manchuria had received a fair share of soybeans during their imprisonment, and were in pretty good physical condition.

The sides of the great battleship loomed high above us as our smaller ship approached. We off-loaded and climbed the ladder; the General was piped aboard and welcomed. After boarding, the General went to the Admiral's cabin while the final preparations were being completed. He was getting taut and, I thought, wanted to be alone. I visited with old friends and chatted with a number from the *Missouri.*

On the veranda deck of the ship, two sides of a square were formed by the signers and the invited dignitaries. One side of the square faced the stern. The adjacent side on the left faced the port side of the ship and Tokyo Bay, with about 40 feet of open deck. The next, facing the bow, was empty, waiting for the Japanese who were to come up a short ladder from the deck below. Cameras to record the ceremony were on a platform partly out over the water on the port side. In the center of the open area was a small oblong table, the height and depth of a card table, with the documents on it and a pen at the side of each.

The Allied representatives were in the group that faced the stern; altogether there were about a hundred people. The General and his Chief of Staff, General Richard Sutherland, stood near the port rail on the right side of the group that faced the stern. Our officers, admirals and Army officers, beginning with the rank of major general, were arranged on the side facing the bay. The officers and men of the *Missouri* were watching from any vantage they could find or were allowed. I stood behind two British admirals at the corner where the two sides joined.

The officers of the *Missouri* with whom I had chatted were warmly expectant. Several of them had volunteered that they were reasonably excited about the day's event and the preparations for it, but when General MacArthur came aboard, they suddenly became aware that they were playing a part in an important historic occasion. Foreign uniforms of representatives of the Allied powers added a touch of pageantry.

The General had not been happy about the Soviets becoming our ally in the Pacific by declaring war on Japan just two weeks before the surrender. He was aware of their great impact on the European theater, and of their awesome losses in the war, but nevertheless thought they were late comers in our theater. He felt they would quickly outnumber us in their Tokyo headquarters, primarily to catch up on the intelligence available, and that they might try to slow down his post-surrender plans with respect to reestablishing the Japanese government.

When we took our places and stood more or less at attention, we all looked expectantly toward the head of a ladder up which the Japanese were to come from the deck below. The General talked quietly with General Sutherland. There were other desultory exchanges, but primarily there was anticipation. Suddenly the major part of a silk hat appeared in the region of the ladder and then almost disappeared. In a second the silk hat with the face of an older Japanese appeared and then sank back, leaving just the hat showing. And then, rather laboriously, the senior Japanese diplomat, Foreign Minister Mamoru Shigemitsu, in silk hat and cutaway, came up to our deck. The sound of his artificial left leg quickly indicated the reason for the antic bobbing. It had been necessary to bring him from a smaller vessel to the *Missouri* in a breeches buoy. He was accompanied by seven men in uniform and two younger civilians. They took their places behind the table, on which lay the two instruments of surrender, and stood without expression. Suddenly Shigemitsu saw a friend directly in front of him and started to smile and greet him warmly until he apparently realized that such a greeting was not appropriate. He assumed a stony face again. The friend that he recognized was the Canadian representative, Colonel Cosgrave (with a severe migraine that morning, for which I had prescribed), who had saved his life on the occasion of his losing his leg. This had occurred when, on a state occasion, a Korean had attempted to assassinate the Emperor with a bomb. I am sure Colonel Cosgrave knew Shigemitsu would be heading the delegation, and that probably was a factor in causing his headache.

To open the ceremony, General MacArthur read a short, positive speech. It was pertinent, not in the least vindictive—a look forward rather than a recounting of the past. It set the tone at a high level for this historic occasion. The depth of his emotion on this occasion was evident to me because of the considerable exaggeration of his usually very mild intention tremor.

General MacArthur had decided to use six pens in signing the two documents. He wanted to honor General Wainwright, who had had to surrender Bataan and Corregidor, and General Percival, the British Commander in Malaya when Singapore fell. Both had been prisoners of war for three years. General MacArthur wanted not only to recog-

The Japanese delegation at the signing of the surrender. Foreign Minister Mamoru Shigemitsu (with top hat and cane) is in the foreground. September 2, 1945.

nize them but also to emphasize the unpreparedness of two great democracies. He wanted to give a pen to West Point, which he had revitalized at a crucial time in its history. One was to go to the War College, and one he wanted for himself. The sixth pen was undesignated. Ben Whipple, Dusty Rhoades, and I had called on all the signers the previous evening and told them there would be an official pen available at the side of each document; that if they wished to keep a pen, they should bring their own.

The General then picked up one of the six pens he had planned to use for the two documents and looked at it. This was the climax, the apex of his military career, his life. There was a hush as though everyone had had that thought. Then slowly and firmly he signed "Douglas." He called General Wainwright forward and gave the first pen to him. He signed "Mac" with the second of his pens and presented it to General Percival. He then signed "Arthur" with the third pen to complete the first document and went to the next one. He signed the Japanese document similarly, laying his pens next to the document.

General MacArthur asked Admiral Nimitz to sign for the United States and then called forward in turn each of our Allies. One of the first to sign was the British Admiral, Sir Bruce Fraser, who took one of the General's pens, signed with it, called forward one of the admirals standing on my toes, and gave it to him. Then he went to the Japanese document, took another of General MacArthur's pens, signed, called forward the other admiral (who was not on my toes), and gave it to him. Reacting to this, one of our officers whispered to me, "Gad, that's carrying Lend-Lease too far." The signing continued in silence except for the varied gaits of the signers and the sound of the motion-picture cameras on the press platform.

"The representative of the Government of Canada will now sign," said General MacArthur, whereupon Colonel Cosgrave, migraine improved but muscles jumpy, virtually leapt to the first document and signed with a flourish, and then to the Japanese document, where he signed on the wrong line. The representative of the Provisional Government of the French Republic followed him, and when he saw that his proper place had been taken, asked where he should sign. General MacArthur and General Sutherland conferred briefly and decided to keep the sequence dictated by protocol and to scratch out the beautifully inscribed names of the remaining countries so that protocol could be followed.

Then it was the Japanese turn. Foreign Minister Shigemitsu stepped forward, took off his hat and laid it beside the document. When he started to sign, the two Chinese took out their handkerchiefs and began to spit noisily into them. This I later learned was an insulting gesture. Shigemitsu looked up, noted the Chinese spitting, perhaps saw a rather awesome grimace on the face of General Blamey's (Australian Commander-in-Chief) Chief of Staff, (who had a noticeable tic under tension), and may have heard the two British admirals, who were both now on my toes, cursing the Japanese out for fair. He picked up his hat, slammed it on his head a bit too hard, and continued to write. When he went to the document to be retained by the Japanese and saw all the scratches beneath the last three names, he raised the question of its legality. General Sutherland came forward, looked at it carefully, and then said, "I'll take care of it." Whereupon he initialed, as the Army does, each correction. This was apparently satisfactory, for the Japanese then finished signing and left the ship—no words, no handshakes.

Signaling the end of the ceremony, our Air Force and Navy flew in formation over the *Missouri* in amazing numbers. It was an impressive show to us, and I'm sure to the Japanese as well.

With the ceremony over, there was a fair amount of handshaking, congratulating, smiling, and talking among friends and allies. The historic moment was over, the tension was released—we should be happy, satisfied, and outgoing. Perhaps we should weep. We then boarded the *Buchanan* and the General started talking with Colonels Reims and Dooley

The signing of the document of surrender on board the battleship
Missouri. September 2, 1945.

about some of our immediate plans in connection with the Japanese demobilization. Back we went to the Customs House Pier and, to my very great surprise, to the office by 11 o'clock in the morning. During this part of the ride, the General was again thoughtful, withdrawn, silent, and volunteered no banal statement about the occasion.

That evening and the next morning, using the appropriate American channels and a fair degree of finesse, Ben and Dusty and I retrieved from the British admirals General MacArthur's two pens and gave two similar ones in substitution.

Thus the General and his staff put behind them four years of war, ended as one always hopes a war will end, with victory for our side. They put war behind them to concentrate on the tremendous job that lay ahead: the creation of a new democracy.

21

Japan: The Beginning of the Democracy

The two million troops were finally moved from the Tokyo area. It was declared demilitarized, and we moved into the Embassy and the Embassy staff buildings. The General established his office in the Dai Ichi building. The staff of the headquarters moved into the Imperial and other hotels and buildings. A new direction and purpose was felt through the GHQ, which had now become the Supreme Command for the Allied Powers. Some of the officers would now have more work, many would be "rotated" home. Most of the enlisted men would be returned to the U.S. Life for all would certainly be more relaxed.

It was time to bring Mrs. MacArthur and Arthur and the others of the household up to Tokyo. This had been a short and a very busy absence for the General, but suddenly he was impatient for Jean. The Embassy would be ready for her, and he could talk new and vitally important problems over with her. He called me into his office one morning and said, "Doc, Dusty is going down to Manila to get Jean and Arthur and the others and bring them up here. I want you to go with him—see if anything needs to be done—and come back soon!"

Flying down with Dusty Rhoades was delightful. We were

The General reads a message in his new office in the Dai Ichi Building in Tokyo, September 6, 1945.

firm friends by now and had much to talk over before we separated, I first, to Cleveland, and he later to Palo Alto.

We stopped in Okinawa for the night. Mrs. MacArthur and the others of the household were ready for us when we reached Manila, and we were soon on our way north. Then came the vicarious pleasure and excitement in viewing again the coast and countryside of Japan with all of them.

The household was settled in a few days. The General was eager and anxious for his first talk with the Emperor, but he apparently wanted to be established before inviting him. It was finally arranged and a date set. General MacArthur had talked with me on several occasions about his plans for the changes he expected to bring about, but as the day approached he didn't discuss the upcoming conversation at all. The war was ours, this was his— at least until well launched.

During the war General MacArthur was a part of a vast structure with which he was familiar. He knew his territory within that structure and could fight for and defend it well. The changes in government that he had been planning for Japan must now have seemed equally important, perhaps more important than the war. However, there was a new milieu. The Department of State would be stepping in to take over at an undefined time. He wanted to have his plans, the ones to which he had given so much thought, in place and running before then. He didn't trust the State Department to understand the combination of military and civilian problems and the importance of the Emperor's authority. In the early phases of his new mission, he protected this opportunity for a great accomplishment by a measure of silence.

We were excited, for we knew that now our Commander-in-Chief would show his statesmanship. We knew how long he had been planning these coming events. This was to be the beginning of a new era for Japan, for us, for the world. It was historic. The day or two before the meeting with Hirohito he was more quiet; he paced more, he tried out a new pipe. On the day when the Emperor was coming he went in to look at the large reception room where he would talk with him, looked at the large davenport facing the wide door, and the chairs flanking it for the interpreters. He asked me to look at it. I thought he moved the furniture around a bit with his eyes, but decided that things were right as they were.

On the spur of the moment, just before the Emperor's arrival, Mrs. MacArthur and I decided to observe this great occasion secretly. We felt somewhat like impish children; we wouldn't ask permission, and she would tell him some time afterward. There was a small balcony about ten feet above the floor level of this large room. Heavy drapes hung across it, with standing room behind them. This is where we could observe and listen, looking right down at the davenport about twenty-five feet away.

At the last moment the General asked me to go out to greet the Emperor when his limousine arrived, and to usher him in. Introductions would probably not be necessary. When we heard the car drive up, I went out to the driveway and opened the car door for him. Out stepped the ruler of the country with which we had been at war these three and a half years, the virtual godhead for its people. He was the authority through which General MacArthur expected to change the feudal political structure of Japan to a democracy. He was a smallish man wearing a cutaway and carrying a top hat, which he briefly put on his head. He resembled closely the pictures of him. I tried to look respectful, polite, welcoming, and friendly, and ushered him into the reception room where General MacArthur was standing. The General took over, showed respect and, while serious, gave a feeling of warmth.

After a short conversation, he indicated where he would like to have the Emperor sit, on the left-hand side of the davenport with his interpreter on the chair next to him, and seating himself with his interpreter at the other end, they began their talk.

I left, ran up the stairs, and joined Mrs. MacArthur; in that dark place behind the drapes we did feel like schoolchildren surreptitiously listening to grownups. We could see well

Emperor Hirohito's first visit to General MacArthur. Photographed in the large hall of the United States Embassy. September 1945.

through the gaps between the drapes, we could hear, and we quickly became intent on the occasion.

The tone of the talk, this first one between these two men, was friendly and as easy as a conversation carried out through interpreters could be. The General thought the Emperor could understand English, but that, in waiting for the interpreter to repeat what he had already heard, he gained a little more time to consider his answer. General MacArthur soon got down to the business of the first cabinet. He was suggesting a cabinet of high military or war-office officials which could continue the complete demobilization of Japan; then the dismantling of the Imperial Japanese staff corps was a little more touchy. The General hinted at succeeding cabinet changes and spoke broadly of his aims for Japan. The meeting lasted about an hour. Through the interpreters the Emperor agreed. The General's tone was one to which agreement seemed appropriate, not the mere acceptance of an order from a conqueror.

Not long after this first conversation between the General and the Emperor, General MacArthur said, "They want me to arrest the Emperor and to hold him for trial as a war criminal." Deeply disturbed and angered, he talked to himself and to me about this. "They don't understand. He was a virtual prisoner of Tojo and the military clique." And, "Why! I can't possibly accomplish the transition without him. He is still our immediate authority." He went on to express his strong conviction about the subject. He stressed that without the Emperor's imperial-divine power over the people, one couldn't accomplish those changes in government so necessary for the future of Japan. Without that succession of cabinets the changes in the financial structure of the country, the agrarian reform, so vital, woman suffrage, and others, could not be brought about. The time was ripe and we must act. These statements fired him up and he went on to discuss what he should do about the orders. He said he could ignore them and that might be the best way, just go ahead with his plans. And then, almost vehemently, he said he could tell them he refused to comply. That would flout them and certainly put his job in jeopardy. He doubted they would discharge him—but reflected, they could. He decided, finally, to ignore it. He could have been talking to himself, for I could offer nothing. But he liked to talk it out in front of me—usually in the car, never in his office.

A week or so later he said they had repeated the order. He did not make it clear whether "they" was the Allies, the President, or the Pentagon. He decided to continue to ignore it, and never mentioned it again.

Soon he was ordered to prohibit our soldiers from fraternizing. He blew up over this one. "Why, our soldiers—in peace—are the best ambassadors any country could have. They are decent and respectful. As in the Philippines, most of them want the feeling of a family, want to get into Japanese homes—bring a bit of food, chocolate or gum for the children. People to people. Think of all the Japanese wartime propaganda we have to undo. Who can do it better? Think of their impact on our relations over the next generation! No, I won't stop it—I'll ignore the order." The order was repeated, but apparently with a little less conviction. The General continued to ignore it and didn't refer to it any more.

Every day as we arrived in the car at the Dai Ichi building where the offices were, there was an increasing crowd of Japanese waiting to see him. They did not try to touch him, they were not autograph hunters; but one couldn't help feeling that they were there more in awe and admiration than out of curiosity. Then one day the General was told through a newspaper advertisement that he would be killed on his way to the office on a certain day. I asked if he wanted to change his schedule, go earlier or later, feeling pretty sure that he wouldn't want to; and he didn't. He wanted to go exactly in his usual pattern, and so we drove to the office through the familiar streets and talked about many things as though no threat had happened, and nothing did happen; except that the crowd was larger in front of the Dai Ichi building, and seemed a bit tense. I also thought I heard a sound—possibly a sigh, not a cheer—when he stepped out of his car.

During my last week with the General he repeatedly talked about the handling of war criminals; trying them. He was concerned that emotion and vindictiveness in certain high quarters might carry this punishment down into the ranks of the regular army. He pointed out several times the group of generals around Hitler. They were politicians first and army officers by decree. Goering was one such; and, using Tojo as an example, he said a similar situation existed in Japan. He once said, "If they drop to the level of professional soldiers, whose aims are of course to win wars, the threat could cause the loss of many more lives. With death sentences facing them, some generals might fight on in sheer desperation, long after there were no reasonable hopes of winning."

With peace between our countries, the General found just as many battles to fight with his higher authorities. When I left, he seemed to be winning them.

22

And Afterwards

In November 1945 it was time for me to return home. I had brought this up in August, but the General had suggested I might like to stay a bit longer. "Doc, you worked your way from Australia to Manila—a hard way, and now you will have a chance to witness the surrender. You would regret it if you should miss that." The Hiroshima and the Nagasaki bombs had been dropped, and he felt the war was over. I stayed, and I was grateful for the experience of these three months. I felt close to the General and I thought he felt warmly towards me.

Came the day of my departure and I went up the hill to the Embassy to say my formal goodbye to the General. The goodbyes had really occurred in conversations over the previous couple of days. There had been times when out of the blue he would ask me what it was like to practice medicine—how would I arrange it—how many worked for or with me. He seemed to raise the question, though he didn't voice it, of how much satisfaction there was to be gained from these doctor-patient associations, and while he understood and sympathized with my need to go home to my family, I had the impression that he thought I should do something other than just seeing patients.

As I entered the large Embassy reception hall, I decided a final salute would be a good touch, though I hadn't used one for some time, but he took matters out of my hands. He grasped my right hand with his, put his left hand on my shoulder, looked at me hard, said, "Thank you, Doc, and I wish you well." Then he was gone, down the steps to his car, and off to work with someone else sitting next to him. The car was soon around a bend and I turned to give a less formal goodbye to Mrs. MacArthur, whom I would now call Jean. It hurt to say goodbye to those two years of increasing closeness to the General and to Jean. We wished each other well, and I am sure we thought we would never meet again. I then went down the same steps and the hill to my quarters, collected my baggage, said goodbye to an empty place, got into a pool car waiting for me, and rode off to the airport as my focus changed to what I had been longing for for almost four years—reunion with my Meg and our family.

But it wasn't the end of our meetings. A few years later when General MacArthur returned from Korea, Jack Sverdrup gave a birthday party for him at the Waldorf which was to become an annual affair attended by the GHQ group with others: George Kenney and some of his Air Force generals, Admiral Kinkaid and some of his admirals and captains, Walter Krueger with a number of his officers, those who had led the fighting or done the planning in the Southwest Pacific Area.

All of us—usually about a hundred or so—who gathered for these reunions, held in the Parquet Room—looked forward to them very much. Every party had an aura originating in admiration, first for General MacArthur and then for many there whose wartime abilities and heroism we all knew. The aura brightened with our consciousness of the presence of a very great leader whom we admired deeply; it was further enhanced by the military dress uniforms with medals, worn by most of the officers still on active duty; by the Army, Air Force, and Navy music; and by some excellent wines. Reminiscences, good conversation, and the awareness of success achieved by most of us, in service and out, enlivened these celebrations.

Jack Sverdrup, Larry Lehrbas, and I would go up to the

MacArthur apartment in the Waldorf, talk with Jean and the General awhile, and then escort him, wearing a tuxedo, down to the party, where he would walk about talking to the officers before dinner. Sometimes he would give a short greeting to the gathering then, sometimes during the after-dinner brandy. Occasionally he delivered a longer talk.

For different reasons three or four of these parties stand out in my memory.

One evening a few years after his return, the General rose when the cigars were being lit and said, "Earlier this evening I was asked what I considered the three worst tragedies that befell us in Korea." Then with vibrant drama he said, "I'm glad he asked me that. I welcome the opportunity to tell you what." He then went on to tell of the success of the Inchon landings (when he had landed far behind the North Korean lines and cut most of their forces off). These landings were successful beyond measure. The enemy was put to rout, cut up, and paralyzed. This great success convinced him that this was the time for those in "higher places" to offer peace—not when we were slugging it out. He continued, "But one week went by, and two weeks went by—and nothing happened. Three weeks passed and the enemy began to regroup and replace, and finally the advantage of our surprise, of the rout and the disorganization, died."

The second event was more tactical, and the third tragic event was at the Yalu: "Charles [Willoughby, his Chief of Intelligence] had told us the enemy was in great force north of the Yalu river." Then he continued to tell us that the Yalu, a large river, had only five bridges across it; that we had undoubted air superiority. Therefore, the obvious strategy was: should the very large number of Red Chinese start to cross the river in force, we could, when we chose, blow up the bridges, cutting their troops off, and then destroy or capture them.

This was a standing order, and so obvious that the enemy must have known it too. So when his officers came and reported to him that the Chinese were indeed crossing the

Yalu in great strength, he told them to go ahead with the planned reaction. "However, I was worried and puzzled. Something was wrong—our enemy was not stupid, he was intelligent, wise, and experienced, and would not enter such an obvious trap. Something was not right." And then his voice became almost hoarse with emotion. "Before our planes could leave the ground, orders came from above telling us that those bridges were sacred, we could not touch them!" And the enemy continued to pour across in great numbers.

On two occasions in the early sixties, General MacArthur was ill on the night of the party. On the first occasion, when we went to his apartment, he looked sick, dull. Although he had a fever, as Jean told us, he insisted on coming to the dinner. He was in uremia and in pain, increasing pain. As he walked slowly down the corridor to the elevator, I wanted very much to take him right down to an ambulance and to the hospital. He joined his comrades, but he didn't finish the evening and had to be rushed to the hospital for an emergency operation. The next year he was in pretty good fettle; he walked to the elevator at his usual good pace, and he mixed and spoke with everybody in the ballroom.

But the following year he was deeply jaundiced; I was told he had been dark yellow on three previous occasions. The condition was obviously due to a large gallstone which was intermittently blocking the flow of bile and causing permanent damage to his liver. His doctor had been unable to persuade him to have an operation. He was definitely sick, and went up to his apartment early.

The following year he appeared well, but that walk down the corridor seemed just a little longer. These severe bouts of illness were taking a toll; his greetings, however, continued firm and cordial, and he spoke by name to all of his old "comrades in arms," as he liked to call us.

On his last birthday, Jack Sverdrup and I went up to get him. His greeting and smile and voice were warm and friendly as usual, but the corridor to the elevator was longer yet, and he didn't say much on the way. Perhaps he was thinking of what he would say on greeting the others. When we arrived in the ballroom, Colonel Stupp, according to what had become custom, called his loud "Attention," to which the tuxedoes as well as the uniforms were glad to respond. The "At ease" was immediately implied. The General walked about ten paces into the room, greeted many guests, and then indicated he would like to say a few words. We gathered about. His voice was soft and gentle as he started: "My comrades in arms"—a short wait as though to organize his thoughts. "I want you to know how much, how very much, I look forward to these occasions, these opportunities to talk with you, be with you. What joy and satisfaction they give me. They are real milestones in my life. I am grateful for each one, and have always looked forward to the next."

He stopped for a change of tone: "I am reminded of a story. It has to do with a Scotsman who was in a crowded compartment on a train from London to Edinburgh. At the first stop he worked his way out over the knees of the others, and they saw him run into the station and get back on board just as the train was pulling out. At the next stop he did the same thing, and when he barely caught the train again on the third stop, one of the passengers said, 'Jock, why are you running into the station at every stop? We have conveniences on the train. Stay aboard.' And Jock looked up and around at the group. He said, 'I'll tell you. I am a very sick man. Yesterday I went to see my doctor, and the doctor told me that my days were few. He said, "Jock, if you want to see your beloved Scotland again, you better start right out and go up there—but mind you, even though you start now you may not make it."—So I'm buying my ticket from station to station.' "

MacArthur entering the Parquet Room of the Waldorf Astoria for his 77th birthday party. January 26, 1958.

Index

Adams, Colonel, 2
Admiralty Islands, 21, 24, 35, 37, 44, 46, 48, 50, 153
Advanced General Headquarters (Philippines), 107
Ah Cheu, 15, 16
Air Force, Japanese, 43, 44
Air Force (United States), 21, 128, 205, 216, 231
Aitape, 24, 35, 44, 49
Aleutian campaign, 19
Allen, Lt. Colonel, 5, 7
Allied
   command, 175
   powers, 211
   prisoners, 131, 135
   representatives, 211
Allies, 1, 135, 206, 210, 215, 228
American
   breakfast, 209
   captives, 144
   division, xiv
   Embassy, (Tokyo), 202, 204, 205, 206, 220, 230
   prisoners, 135
   troops, 135, 198, 202
Americans, 1, 80, 135, 136, 139, 145, 203, 205, 206, 210; *see also* United States
Angeles, 132
APA, 49
Army, Japanese, 95
Army, Philippine, xii
Army, (United States), 6, 9, 12, 13, 16, 40, 48, 59, 80, 88, 92, 104, 112, 119, 163, 164, 205, 216
Army (U.S.)
   Engineers, 160
   Medical Corps, 82
   nurse, 13

officers, 211
physician, 4
rations, 4
secret code, 3
Secretary of the, 196
troops, 11
Asia (southeast), xii, 103
Atabrine, 10, 12
Atsugi
   Air Base, 198
   airdome, 195
Aussies, 177, 178
Australia, xii, xiv, 3, 6, 8, 10, 14, 21, 61, 81, 91, 165, 166, 175, 185, 204, 230
Australian
   Commander-in-Chief, 216
   Imperial Division, 172
   longshoremen, 175
   soldiers, 178
   sovereignty, 175
   Telephone building, 12, 38, 42
   troops, 171, 175
Australians, xii, 1, 3, 38, 172, 175, 205

Bacolod, 33
Baguio, 112
Bailey bridges, 160
Balikapapen, 177
Ballentine, Admiral John J., 209
BAR (Browning Automatic Rifle) men, 125, 140, 143, 145, 146, 148, 150
Barbey, Admiral Daniel E., 23, 59
Bataan, xii, 84, 88, 127, 130, 135, 144, 145, 146, 150, 151, 158, 205, 212
Bataan, the, 19, 21, 35, 39, 62, 197
Bertrandas, Colonel Victor E., 21, 35
Biak Island, 43, 54
Bilibid Prison, 131, 134, 135, 205
   starvation in, 135
"Bing Bang" Bong, 33

236